The Unfaithfuls

Norma Iris Pagan Morales

ISBN 978-1-959895-62-6 (paperback)
ISBN 978-1-959895-61-9 (ebook)

Printed in the United States of America

WESTPOINT
PRINT AND MEDIA

Acknowledgement

This novel is dedicated to my sister, Adelin Pagan Morales.
She was the only one that always praised my work.
Adelin is gone; however, she lives deep in my heart.

Overview

What could the problem be? I kept thinking when I suddenly remembered what occurred between her husband and I the previous night.

Could she have found out? How did she get to know about it?

My adrenaline began pumping uncontrollably. I'm finished. I don't want to go back to that life of poverty. Just this one chance I was given, and I messed up.

Contents

Chapter 1

Johnny

Johnny was my aunt's husband, and I have been living with her family for quite some time. A period of almost 2 months. She had already given birth to three kids.

Her first son was within my age range... I was 19 and Tommy was 17 and very handsome too, Steven was 15 while the last born, Bobby was 8 years old.

They were all males and overly pampered, in the sense that they couldn't take good care of the home whenever their mom, Jean was away.

That was where I, Elsie, came into the picture. I was the extra helping hand needed to assist with the house chores especially when Aunt Jean was away on her company trips.

She promised to take full responsibility for funding my education as far as I was going to help her take of the family whenever she's absent.

Due to the nature of her job, she was never around. She keeps moving from one project to the another... she needed a house help but she refused hiring one.

Because of the evils occurring in the country, she thought it better that a relative should help by taking care of the house and kids.

It was a golden opportunity for me and my family because I come from a very poor background...a scenario where my both parents are uneducated.

We fed from hand to mouth....it was that bad. My parents struggled to make ends meet and it was very difficult to cater for our education.

With every single passing day, the situation kept worsening.

So, without hesitation, I immediately took the opportunity to help Aunt Jean. Who knows maybe when I graduate from the University.... I may be the one to elevate my family from poverty.

My parents were overjoyed, at least the burden of one child had been lifted from them.

I worked very hard for my aunt and her family. Whatever chore she asked me to do, I did it thoroughly to the best of my human capacity. I knew my purpose there and concentrated on it. That was until my aunt's husband started making passes at me.

Whenever Johnny came home from work, he would always ask about my well-being. He would often ask if I had eaten and how I spent my day.

I was so free and open-hearted with him. I didn't take any of his profound kindness towards me seriously as I took him to be a lovely and caring father who would take care of other children just like his own. I looked at him as a father figure.

In fact, we got so close to the extent I started calling him "dad" while he called me his baby. My aunt wasn't aware of all these happening. It didn't take long before the sugar-coated kindness and affection revealed it's hidden agenda.

Johnny would hold my hands and sometimes even ask me to hug him. I still took it as a normal thing not until one evening when I was preparing dinner for the family.

I was in the kitchen while Aunt Jean was just in the sitting room watching the news. Her husband Johnny walked in....

"My baby, how have you been" he asked in a soft tone.

"I'm fine dad" I replied, almost immediately.

"I missed you today, didn't you miss me " he asked with a smile on his face.

2

I was so naive that I still didn't know what was going on, so I replied, "I missed you, daddy".

I noticed that he kept staring at me while I prepared the food. The next thing he did left me speechless. I noticed Johnny bringing his face towards mine.

"What is he trying to do". It can't be what I'm thinking.

I remained frozen at the spot as he brought his lips towards mine.

Instinctively, in a quick reflex, I tilted my head backwards away from his. I was more than surprised. Was he in his right senses. What was wrong with him?

He must have realized himself as he quickly brought his face backwards and immediately left the kitchen in a somewhat shameful manner.

I still didn't believe he tried to kiss me. I was shocked. I mean, his wife was sitting there in the living room. A lot of thoughts kept racing through my mind.

What if I didn't shift back? What if we had kissed?

What if my aunt who just gave me the hope of a brighter future caught me kissing her husband in her own kitchen? What if?

Chapter 2

Elsie's Confusion

I still couldn't stop thinking about what followed between me and my aunt's husband the previous night. I could only wonder if he really meant his actions or maybe he was under the influence of alcohol.

It was the next morning and as usual I woke up early to start my chores; I had done the dishes, swept the house, and even prepared breakfast. I had already prepared Steven and Bobby. Tommy was taking them to school.

Aunt Jean would be leaving very early for work today, so I had to be fast as possible.

After about an hour, my aunt had woken up. She asked her first son, Tommy who was already done with secondary school to call for me.

"My mom said you should meet her IMMEDIATELY" he said in an urgent tone.

His sentence frightened me. Why would she ask me to meet her immediately??

What could the problem be? I kept thinking when I suddenly remembered what occurred between her husband and I the previous night.

Could she have found out? How did she get to know about it?

My adrenaline began pumping uncontrollably. I'm finished. I don't want to go back to that life of poverty. Just this one chance I was given, and I messed up.

I walked like a snail as I slowly dragged my legs to the sitting room. My aunt was sitting on the couch. I became very uncomposed as the throbbing of my heart increased.

"Elsie" she said drawing my attention.

"I don't want you to be at home all day doing nothing, so I decided you should learn a skill." I was relieved finally hearing her speak. "I've registered a one-year tailoring program for you with the tailoring shop in the street next door. The lady who owns the place is the tailor. I give her my clothes to fix all the time. She's very good at what she does.

So, when you learn from her, you'll be very good at tailoring and maybe even better than her."

Oh, my goodness. This was unbelievable, I was as happy as someone who just won a lottery. Wow my aunt must be a very kindhearted person. After promising to further my education, she still thought it wise for me to learn a skill. I was amazed because such people are rare.

Having any sexual affairs with her husband would be a very wicked and cruel act, something I can never do.

But how certain was I......

Since I did my S.A.T. exams, I have been at home almost every day.

The chores at home had become too much for me. I pressured my mom to get a housekeeper to help us.

My mom came back home one evening with one of my cousins. She said her name was "Esther."

I couldn't recognize her anymore. Last saw each other was about nine years ago during a burial ceremony in the village. Esther was a very hard-working and well-mannered beautiful young lady, but I had noticed this closeness, this bond between my dad and her.

I always knew my dad to be very wild. He was never a faithful husband, matters became even worse when he became a lecturer!

He would try to have an affair with any beautiful lady he sees during classes and my mom never knew about it. I was aware of most of his unrestrained deeds. I would always eavesdrop on his calls and when I became suspicious, I took it to my heart to find out his phone password.

Luckily, I succeeded but the messages I saw on his phone that day were terrible, I can never forget, and I won't want my mom to know about it because it would leave her completely broken.

So, I had to keep all these secrets to myself. My dad was a typical hypocrite at work, in the environment, and even in the church. Everyone knew him as a saint… but he was far from it.

I had started getting worried, I just hoped he had not brought his indiscriminate sexual attitude into the home, but I was wrong.

I greeted Uncle Johnny, and he answered in his usual friendly manner as if nothing ever happened. I was quite happy that it was over. But my relief was cut short when Uncle Johnny started complaining of back ache and body pains.

Surprisingly, he asked me to come and massage his back. In his room. He continued bleating about how he had been feeling body pains since yesterday.

I needed to decline his request but how do I go about it, how would it sound if my aunt hears I disobeyed her husband. Besides it was just a simple massage.

So, resentfully I knocked on his room door. "Come in" Johnny replied with excitement visibly written all over his voice. I opened the door and entered only to see Uncle Johnny lying on the bed almost naked with a short pair of boxers…

I closed the door behind me and gently walked to the bed. "I'm here sir" I said with my head bent towards the ground as I stood shyly before him.

"Just open my wardrobe and bring out the Vaseline, that is what you'll use to massage me."

I quickly did as he said. I was uncomfortable and I didn't want anyone to see me in his room. I needed to leave soon if not it could result into a serious problem.

The fan whirled above my head in a rhythmic manner. Vaseline was all over my hands now as I slowly worked my palms on Uncle Jonny's leg.

He insisted that I start the massage with his legs. I added more Vaseline to my hands as I rubbed them together to massage his shin.

I didn't know if he did it intentionally or it was a mistake. Because after a while, Uncle Johnny raised his lap a bit exposing his thighs and a little part of his sac was now visible.

I immediately shifted my gaze. That was when I knew it was a well-constructed script as he raised his thigh even higher exposing some part of his thing. He was literally seducing me. The tension on me was becoming too much. I wanted to vanish away that instant. I hoped that someone would eventually come back but my hopes were dashed when I remembered that Tommy was not even at home.

"Ohhh…ahh… yeah…umm, that's the spot."

Thirty minutes later, we were done.

This man meant business; he kept releasing soft moans throughout as I massaged him. I covered the container and dropped it back into the wardrobe.

"Thank you very much" he said appreciatively.

"Thank you, sir," I replied.

I had stopped calling him dad since the incident in the kitchen that night.

Finally, it was over but not for long. With almost every passing day, my aunt's husband kept feeling "body pains" and I kept on massaging him. It suddenly became like a routine and normal something for me.

I came out from Uncle Johnny's room after massaging him one afternoon to meet Tommy who was standing just in front of the door. I immediately became scared; I just hope he isn't thinking something else. He gave me a kind of "am watching you" look and left the place.

You wouldn't need an angel to tell you that he had already began suspecting that something was going on between me and Johnny. Wouldn't it be better if I just opened to him and stop him from thinking I have anything to do with his dad?

I needed someone to confide in, I couldn't tell my aunt because she might end up sending me back to prevent any further occurrences.

But if I tell his son, how would he feel, to know that his dad has been trying to cheat on his wife with his cousin. I didn't know what action to take. I walked up to where he was and decided it was time to spill the beans.

"Tommy" I said "Umm… I want to tell you something" I stuttered.

"What's that" he urged on

"Hmm… I just don't know what you reaction will be."

"It's fine, you can go on" Tommy said boldly.

I couldn't speak, it was like my lips were suddenly bound together with glue. I didn't know what to say or where to start from, what if he doesn't believe me. I was still comporting myself when he spoke.

"Is it about my dad? it's alright you can tell me anything" he said.

Immediately I was relieved of the pressure on me and told him everything that had being going on. But to my utmost surprise, he seemed calm and unperturbed. There was no speck of shock in him.

It felt like he was already expecting such from his dad. I was as eased as a fishpond, at least someone else knew what was going on. I could now go to bed with peace of mind.

Chapter 3

Misled

The following morning, I was woken up by the piercing sound of my phone alarm, I got up, said a short prayer, and stood up to begin my duties.

I walked up to the sitting room, and I realized I wasn't the only one awake.

I stopped and greeted Uncle Johnny who was with a bottle of water which he must have probably gotten from the kitchen.

"Good morning, sir"

"Good morning my dear, how are you."

"I'm fine thank you sir."

I was still in my nighties and my bobs and tips were terribly visible through my night gown.

"Hope you slept well" he asked glancing at my upper chambers.

"Yes sir" I answered.

"It's alright then" he said as he walked passed me and intentionally brushed his hands against my bobs.

My uncle Johnny tried different approach to touch me or to be alone with me. I was really feeling strange about the whole situation. If I said anything, that meant that was going to be sent home. I didn't want to do that. I just suffered all alone....

Chapter 4

Aunt Jean

"Hope you slept well" he asked glancing at my upper chambers. Yes sir" I answered.

"It's alright then" he said as he walked passed me and intentionally brushed his hands against my bobs.

"Huhh" I gasped instantly in shock. I was stunned, now this man has taken things too far. He ignored me acting like he wasn't aware of what just happened as he instantly went to his room.

It was no mistake, it appeared he was deliberately trying to make me know he wanted to have extramarital affairs with me, but he didn't want to use his words. He preferred using signs.

It's a Monday morning and the beginning of a new week. I couldn't wait to resume at my place of apprenticeship. Aunt Jean also had me enrolled for evening Marketing lessons, at least I wouldn't be at home always with her husband, who was on his monthly leave.

She would be busy throughout this week due to the preparation for the launching of the new branch her company just planted.

She worked in a multinational industrial firm. She earns huge amounts of money every month. Her working environment was also very good too, but it limited the role she had to play as a mother.

She had very little time to spend with her family, but she sure made her presence felt whenever she was around.

She is a very hard-working and caring woman. What I cherished most about her was the fact that she easily felt pity for others, and she used her money to enrich the lives of the less privileged.

I began learning the tailoring skill my aunt paid for today. The woman who owned the shop seemed to be a very nice woman. She put me through on the basics and explained everything to me in the simplest of terms.

The talking part was easy, but the practical part was the exact opposite just like they say " it is easier said than done."

I arrived home that afternoon terribly exhausted. Everyone was at home apart from my aunt, Tommy had brought the kids back from school while Uncle Johnny was probably in his bedroom.

I had not even started the evening lessons and I was already getting worked up. It wasn't going to be easy for me to manage the tailoring, house chores and lessons all together.

I was highly fatigued and just needed to jump into my bed and sink into the coolness that it brings. It was barely five minutes since I lay on the bed when I was woken up from my nap by the sound of a soothing, calm voice.

"Elsie! Wake up, my dad has been calling you."

I opened my eyes to see Tommy who was now tapping my shoulders.

"What's the matter" I asked with a fatigued voice.

"My dad has been calling you since, he wanted you to follow him to the supermarket to get some things."

"Hmm" I breathed deeply.

What is this man's problem, I haven't even slept for up to five minutes and he wants me to go on another errand with him. Why does he keep pestering me? Right now, what I needed was rest!

I quickly put one of my short gowns, it was a bit worn but was still manageable.

My mom had gotten it for me two years ago for the Christmas celebration.

I met Uncle Johnny in the passage,

"Good afternoon, sir" I greeted.

"Good afternoon, please hurry up let's get some things your aunt asked me to get from the supermarket" Johnny said hurriedly and left to the garage.

I came outside and waited for him outside his car, he then signaled me to join him inside. I hopped unto his 2023 Range Rover Velar. Wow! the interior was a sight to behold. From the seats to the floor mats to the steering and the navigation system was absolutely mind blowing. The air conditioner was on and that made the car even more classic.

It was the perfect environment for me to relax.

"How was work today" Johnny asked.

"Fine sir" I replied.

"You look tired, it must have been very stressful."

"Yes sir, tailoring isn't actually as easy as I thought" I said.

"How about we stop at a restaurant to get you something to eat?" He said smiling.

"Ok sir" I said, I couldn't turn down the offer just like that.

One more thing; please stop addressing me as sir. You can call me dad or Johnny.

"I'm sorry but Johnny sounds disrespectful. I prefer calling you dad."

"As you wish" he said with a smirk on his face.

After about 20 minutes we arrived at the restaurant, it was one of the biggest in New York. Well decorated to the class of the times with very friendly staffs.

I immediately concluded that the food here would be very expensive. Uncle Johnny ordered a plate of rice and chicken, and I asked for the same thing because I was divided between two minds after seeing the cumbersome menu.

We chatted during the meal, about my family, social life, and a lot of other things I can't recall. I had a nice time, and it was a great way to relax after a hectic day.

By the time we were done, it was already late, the time ran fast. We hurried down to get the things from the supermarket. It was getting dark, so we had to be very swift.

As if the meal at the restaurant wasn't enough Uncle Johnny also got me a perfume worth $85.00. The scent was heavenly!

I asked him why he was being extra caring and loving to me, but my question surprisingly threw him off balance. It took him a few seconds to provide an answer.

"I... I... just want to see you happy and smiling that's all" he said.

I didn't care, after all I wasn't a kid anymore. I knew very well what he wanted. Aside that, I had started to feel comfortable around him, I began enjoying his company... I don't know how to explain it, but I think I'm beginning to like Uncle Johnny...

Chapter 5

No Concentration

Tommy just couldn't concentrate while he played a video game in his room. He kept wondering why his dad and Elsie were not back by now.

It has been almost two hours since they left to the supermarket. On a normal circumstance they ought to have been back by now. Even his mom was already back from work while they were still on their way.

What could be delaying them? Could they have gone somewhere else? He kept on soliloquizing. He became even more worried as he remembered what had been going on between both.

Could the outing have been planned? Could it be that Elsie had finally surrendered to his dad's seduction?

"Hmm" he whispered to himself. He has been tolerating all these nonsenses just because he doesn't want his parents' marriage to get broken. He can't afford seeing his mom in tears. Life wouldn't be easy on his siblings and him if anything bad happens to his parents' marriage.

If anything should occur between Elsie and his dad, that would be the last time he would keep silent. Despite his gentleness he can be very threatening and if eventually anything happens, he might end up doing something very stupid.

For his cousin, Elsie, it would be a huge shock to her the length he would go to make her life miserable.

I had sunk deep in thoughts when I was jolted up by the loud sound of the car's horn. I got up from my chair and looked downstairs through my room window.

My dad's car drove in as Musa opened the gate. I was able to see clearly with the help of the high energy light bulbs in our compound. Oga welcome, welcome sir, your boy Dey loyal sir" Musa said raising his both hands in the air with a very wide and absurd smile.

He kept on hailing my dad hoping to get some change to promote his drinking habit. Dad stepped down from the car while Elsie went to get the things they bought from the trunk. I couldn't help but notice the way they were talking and smiling. It irritated me. I couldn't wait to speak to Elsie.

It was already dark when they arrived. They hurried back home as fast as possible. They must have spent a lot of time since aunty Jean was already back from work.

Elsie was a bit startled because she never expected her aunt to be back so early compared to prior times.

"Good evening ma" Elsie quickly greeted her trying to reduce the uneasiness I was feeling.

"How are you?" Aunt Jean asked

"Fine ma"

"You spent a lot of time at the supermarket…" she said expecting a reply from me.

Elsie couldn't just go ahead and tell her that she and her husband stopped at the restaurant. She would make her feel suspicious.

So, she told her that there was heavy traffic on our way.

She didn't ask any further questions as she was busy arranging some of her paperwork.

Elsie was just about leaving when she inquired about my tailoring classes. She wanted to know if I had started learning the tailoring skill.

"Yes ma" I said, "thank you very much for all you have done for me ma. May God bless you deeply ma, I am very grateful" I said bending my knees forward as a sign of respect.

"Don't bother yourself my dear, it's nothing" she replied with a smile on her face.

I was in my room when I heard a hard knock on the door. I sluggishly got up and opened the door.

It was Tommy.

"Hi Tommy, what's up" I asked but he didn't reply it was obvious he was angry about something.

"What's the matter" I inquired looking concerned.

"What are up to!!" he thundered.

"What are you doing with my father!!!"

"Tommy, you have to calm down let's go inside, we can't be discussing such at the doorpost" I pleaded.

I entered inside the room, and he followed me, but he left the door open.

"Now will you please answer my question??"

"Look, I don't know what you're insinuating but nothing is going on between me and your dad.

"Then why did you guys spend more than two good hours to just get something from the supermarket."

"I… I… I was very hungry and stressed so he said we should get something to eat at the restaurant.

"You went to the restaurant with my dad??" My statement seemed to have infuriated him the more.

"When last did he take me to the restaurant?!" Frank asked rhetorically.

He was enraged and fuming in annoyance.

"And you told my mom there was heavy traffic!"

I didn't know what to say to calm down his nerves. He was absolutely annoyed.

"Please you don't have to be worried about that, nothing will ever happen between us. I am fully aware of what I am doing. Besides that, I have boundaries which I take very seriously."

"That's none of my business, but one thing is sure if I you ever sleep with my father it'll be the biggest mistake of your life.

"Biggest mistake of whose life?" was the next thing we heard from the door. We were stunned as we shifted our gaze towards the door and behold it was Aunty Jean.

Chapter 6

The Mistake

"Biggest mistake of whose life?" was the next thing we heard. We were overwhelmed as we shifted our gaze towards the door and behold it was aunty Jean.

I was visibly shaking as my aunt's voice pierced through my heart. Tommy caused all this, if he had just listened to me and behaved a little mature, we wouldn't be in this mess.

The best I could do at this moment was to just hope and pray that Aunt Jean had not been listening to our conversation the whole time.

"What were you both talking about? Tommy what will be the biggest mistake of her life?" Aunt Jean questioned. Tension filled the air as everyone kept mute.

"I'm I not talking to human beings" Aunt Jean said raising her voice.

"We…we…we were discussing our future ambitions when Elsie suggested taking up singing as a career, that was why I told her it would be the biggest mistake of her life because she has a terrible voice" Tommy said.

"Huhh" I sighed within myself. I was very much relieved, a huge part of me felt he would tell his mom everything, so I was very surprised when he covered up for me.

"Is that so?" she asked in a doubtful manner.

"Yes" we chorused.

"Well, that's not why I'm here… Elsie here's $30.00, it should be enough to do your hair. So please do that tomorrow."

"Thank you, ma, thank you very much."

"You're welcome" Aunt Jean I said as she left us.

I immediately shifted my gaze to Tommy who was staring at the floor.

"Thank you for covering up for me" I said in a sober and childish tone.

"Umm… I'm sorry…for the way I talked to you earlier. I was acting based on the anger I felt at that time, and I just wanted you to be careful around my dad."

"It's okay, I'm very sorry too for going to the restaurant with your dad. But you don't have to be worried about me, in a few months' time I'll be twenty. So, I know how to take care of myself."

"Elsie, it seems like you still don't get me, my dad is ready to have sex with any available lady. That is whenever he wants her. He can do anything to have that person.

Even at the University where he works, he is ready to undo any female student just to taste what's between their legs even if it means failing them on purpose!"

"Hmm… that's serious. I'll try my best to be extra careful with him."

"You better be" Tommy said in a rather caring voice as he walked out of my room."

The following morning, I was woken up by the usual buzzing of my 5 am alarm. I managed to reach my phone and put it off. I still felt very sleepy.

Just then a message notification popped up on my Nokia handset. It was an old model of Nokia. A very cheap but strong phone. I had used it for close to five years, but it was still alright.

I continued smiling till I was done reading the message. It was from my boyfriend, Charlie. He was very fond of sending me romantic messages in the morning.

But the messages he sent today were different, he sent sexy messages about how long he had missed my bobs and my thing. Charlie was always very naughty, so I wasn't very surprised.

He kept talking about how he couldn't wait to see me and feel himself inside me. Anyone reading the message would probably feel I had had sex a lot of times, but reverse was the case.

I have never tasted sex, although there were instances where I almost lost my virginity, I had no idea what sex felt like.

This was the reason I was confident nothing would happen between me and Tommy's dad. I never fancied keeping my virginity this long, but it just happened and losing it to a man old enough to be my dad wasn't the way I wanted it to end.

I wanted it to be an amazing unforgettable experience with someone.

Later that day, Uncle Johnny was back. I could hear the roaring of his car from outside the compound. I avoided him like a plague through-out the day. The only time we spoke to each other was when I greeted him.

He later went out that afternoon. I earlier overheard him on the phone speaking to someone. It sounded like he had an appointment that would bring him a lot of money.

Everyone was at home including aunty Jean.

Uncle Johnny walked in smiling seriously with some nylon bags and an envelope.

Aunty Jean was in the sitting room. "Welcome honey" she said.

"Thank you" replied as he gave her the envelope in his hand signaling her to read it. She screamed joyously; it must be very good news I thought to myself.

"Where is Elsie, where are the kids. Call them let's celebrate" Uncle Johnny gave a joyful laugh as he brought out some drinks and plates of food from the bags he was holding.

Everyone came out see what the joyful was all about.

"Drink everyone, daddy has just made more money" Uncle Johnny said laughing joyously.

It was an awesome night, we enjoyed ourselves and ate to satisfaction. I can't remember the last time I ate this much food. I was absolutely overstuffed.

Once we were finished, I packed the plates and carried them to the kitchen.

As I walked, I noticed someone was following me. I turned back. It was Uncle Johnny. I was frightened at his sight.

"Jesus...sir you scared me" I said.

"I'm sorry my dear, I never meant to scare you. I just wanted to check up on you."

"So how was your day?" He asked.

"Fine, thank you sir."

"Ok that's good. You see; I just wanted to let you know that if there is anything you need, I mean anything at all within my capacity you should do well to let me know, ok?"

"Ok sir but you don't need to bother yourself, I don't have any pressing needs."

"Are you sure, what about your phone? Don't you think you need a new one?" He questioned.

"Hmm... I guess I do, I'm tired of my phone and I'll be very delighted if you can get me a new one. My phone is very old, and it even started malfunctioning. I will be more than happy if you can get me a new phone sir."

It's alright then..." he said. "Thank you very much sir... I'm grateful."

I was overwhelmed with joy until he spoke again. "I can get you any model of phone you want as long as you do what I tell you..."

Chapter 7

The Bribery

"I can get you any model of phone you want as long as you do what I tell you" Uncle Johnny said once again. He walked away from the kitchen leaving me stunned.

I couldn't believe my ears; this man really doesn't give up. So, he wants to prey on my desires and use them to exploit me.

Does he really think that I'm a kid who he can just trick easily. It seems he doesn't know the kind of harsh and wayward environment I was born into. It's just by God's grace that I didn't turn sour.

Since he's ready to play games, I'll let him know that I can play better than him.

Since he is ready to spend money, I will help him very generous to spend it! I said as I walked boldly to my room.

I think I have finally gotten a hold on this girl. I don't even know what's so special about her that she has being playing hard to get. At this young age, she has constantly refused to yield herself to me.

Nevertheless, I know I will get her, since she lived from the village it shouldn't take a lot to get her feeling intimate affections towards me.

I needed to get some sleep, tomorrow I'll make my move. My wife was already in bed, but she was yet to fall asleep.

The expression that beamed up her face when she saw me indicated that she must have been waiting for me to enter the room.

I took off the blue polo shirt and shorts I was putting on, sat on the bed and was about lying down when my wife spoke to me.

"Johnny"

"Yes, what is it?" I asked.

"Johnny, there's something I've being really bothered about, and I wanted us to discuss."

"Okay, go on" I said.

"Johnny, it has been very long since we last had sex, every single night you just leave me dry and go to bed. I have confronted it for too long and I can't take it any longer. Such a thing isn't good for us as a couple; it could lead to extramarital affairs…you know."

"So??"

"Johnny I am a woman; you can't just leave me like. We hardly have sex with each other and even if we do it's occasionally. The worst part is…"

"It's enough! Jean, I need rest!" I quickly interrupted her from finishing whatever thing she was about to say.

"I've been busy all through the day. Can't you see that I'm tired, Jean, I am very tired. Remember I have a very important meeting tomorrow, you're supposed to let me rest instead you're busy talking about sex??"

"Johnny that's what you always say, that's what you always say! Everyday I'm around and talk to you concerning this matter that's always when you need rest.

Johnny let me know; this habit you're putting up it is not healthy for our marriage at all. It isn't good. I just don't know why you keep acting as if we're not yet married or something.

Aside that, you know I am a lady sometimes a lady like me needs good hot sex with her husband not all these ones you are doing."

"See Jean that's your business, right now I don't need sex what I need is sleep. Allow me to sleep, we'll do that good hot sex some other time; not today please" I said as I covered myself with the comforter.

Chapter 8

Elsie and Uncle Johnny

Today was another very hectic day, this tailoring work isn't easy at all. My madam bombarded me with work after work. It's either I'm cutting the material, or I'm ironing or I'm weaving the clothes or I'm even walking under the scorching sun to get sewing items from a store that sells sewing materials very far from the shop.

It is always chaotic and today was not an exception. After taking a shower and eating my lunch the next thing to do was to call Charlie.

I dialed his number as I waited patiently for him to pick up.

"Hello, my love how are you doing?"

"I'm okay, how are you" I asked.

"I'm fine, I've missed you a lot" he said.

"I missed you more babe" I replied.

"So, when will you come to see me, I can't stop thinking about you."

"I'm not sure if I'll be able to visit any time soon."

"Hmm…okay then, at least we would be talking on the phone."

"So how is your aunt's place, you go done fat finish " he jokingly said in his strong creole accent.

"Everything is fine, my aunt is really trying. The only problem I'm facing now is her husband."

"What did he do? Hope he is not beating my wife."

"No" I chuckled.

"It's something else… I don't even know how I'm going to explain it."

"Ah ah, go on. Have you forgotten you are talking to your love you don't need to start thinking of how you'll explain it."

"Fine, from the way he has being behaving I think he wants me to… I'm sorry please can you cut the call he's calling me."

"Who is calling you" Charlie asked.

"Uncle Johnny, my aunt's husband, please cut the call let me answer him."

"So, you want me to cut the call because of him??"

"Babe just cut the call so that I can pick his, I call you later." Charlie hung up before I could even finish, I just hope he isn't angry with me.

"Hello Elsie, how are you."

"I'm fine sir."

"Please I need you to come meet me at the roundabout."

"But sir, I'm about leaving the house for my evening lessons.

"Just forget about evening lessons for today, okay? I'll be waiting for you; I need you to hurry up and please wear something nice" he said as he hung up the call.

What is this man's problem? Why does he want me to meet him somewhere on the road. I hope he doesn't have a hidden motive.

"Drop me!" I said to the tricycle driver who stopped the vehicle for me to alight. I gave him the fare and he quickly drove away.

I kept looking around, but I couldn't find Uncle Johnny, he was the one who asked me to come here but he has not even arrived. I was still checking around when I saw Uncle Johnny's car parked across the road.

He had seen me also and began waving at me to cross over.

I crossed, opened the car door, and joined him at the front seat.

"Good evening, sir" I said.

"Evening dear" he replied softly.

"Sir I'm sorry to ask but why did you ask me to meet you here?" I said trying hard not to sound disrespectful.

"I just wanted us to go out, relax, eat something, and have a wonderful evening. I hope you don't mind?"

"No, it's okay with me" I smiled at him.

It was obvious Uncle Johnny was unaware of who he was dealing with, I'll make sure I exploit a fortune out of him.

The thick silence was broken as Uncle Johnny spoke.

"Elsie, do you know you're actually very beautiful" he said trying to sound romantic.

"You have a very radiant smile that gives me goosebumps whenever I'm around you" he said smiling.

"Wow" I smiled forcing a blush.

You're just deceiving yourself I said within me.

"Has anyone ever told you such before" he asked.

"No, no one has."

"Does that mean you don't have a boyfriend?"

"No" I lied.

"Really??"

"Yes sir, why would I lie to you" I said.

I want to ask you a personal question, I don't know how it would sound to you but have you had sex before?"

I was stunned by his question, why would he be asking me something so personal. He didn't even mind how his question would make me feel.

"No sir, I haven't"

"You must be joking" he said almost laughing.

"I'm not sir, I'm a virgin."

"Are you serious??" He said looking very surprised.

"Yes sir, I've never had sex before" I answered.

If you're telling the truth, then I must say you are missing a lot."

"What I'm I am missing?" I asked looking very confused.

"Don't worry, I'll show you" Uncle Johnny said.

He drove in silence for about five minutes until he came to a halt in front of a hotel.

"What are we doing here sir, I thought you said we were just wanted to relax and have something to eat.

"My dear you don't have to be paranoid, I lodged here so I can just have a mini vacation. Away from family, work, and all that.

This is where I come most of the time, it is a very big hotel. Besides, they have a bar and restaurant in case you need something to eat. In fact, why don't I show you around. Trust me you'll love it.

"Hmm" I sighed. "Okay then"

It was indeed a very big and luxurious hotel. The Hilton hotel which was boldly crafted above the building. It was a classic five-star hotel, only the reception was a sight to behold.

We went to the restaurant, the swimming pool, and the bar. It was just so classy.

"This man has class " I thought to myself.

We ordered some drinks, and I was enjoying myself. It was like I was in heaven already.

"Are you shy?" He asked.

"No sir, am not."

"I thought we've agreed that you should stop calling me sir."

"I'm sorry sir... I'm sorry dad."

"Better he said, you've enjoyed yourself today, isn't it?"

"Yes, thank you very much" I replied.

"The hotel is elegant, right?"

"Yes, it's very amazing."

I was still drinking my juice when Uncle Johnny asked me to follow him to the third floor. We entered the elevator, after a few seconds we were on the third floor. I felt unsettled as Uncle Johnny cupped his hands into mine. He led me to a passage with different rooms, we kept on walking until he stopped in front of a door written room 406 that was when I realized we were in front of the room where he lodged!!

Chapter 9

The Bate

As soon as I saw it, it stuck to my brain like iron does to a magnet. "Please what are we doing here?" I asked him.

"You see I lodged here for today and tomorrow so this is where I'll spend the night" he said as he unlocked the door.

He opened the door with a card rather than a key. It was indeed a very fancy hotel.

Uncle Johnny entered the room and signaled me to do likewise. It was very dark and hot inside.

He then inserted the card into a slot and suddenly the lights came up and the air conditioner was turned on.

The brightness of the lights revealed the beauty of the room in its magnificence.

"Wow!" I heard myself say.

This is luxury at its best. The room was very spacious and well furnished. It had a king size bed, a 42-inch plasma tv and an extremely soft-looking sofa.

There was also this very beautiful painting of a woman carrying a bottle with her little child just beside her.

It was amazing and to think that the arrangements were made extraordinarily perfect was just so mind blowing. I could only wonder how much Uncle Johnny had spent.

"It's wonderful, don't you think?" he asked.

"Yeah; it's absolutely amazing" I said.

Our conversation was short-lived as it got interrupted by the beeping sound of his phone ringtone. I took a quick peek at his phone and Sandy was displayed on his phone screen.

I noticed how he acted when the call came in, he didn't want to pick up at first. I didn't know if it was my presence that made him behave that way but after much hesitation, he answered the call.

"Hello... yes. Ok, not now please. In like thirty minutes time.

Ok then I'll be expecting you" he said and ended the call.

"I'm sorry for the interruption, I would have loved you to stay for longer, but you need to go home before my wife gets back from work" he said. I felt like he no longer wanted me around.

"Ok then, I should be leaving" I said.

Even I had started getting restless and my body itched to leave the room.

"You don't have to be bothered; you can come see me again tomorrow."

"Tomorrow?... I'm sorry sir but that won't be possible because tomorrow is a Saturday. I don't have any excuses to leave the house since there'll be no evening lessons. Apart from that aunty Jean would also be at home."

"Don't worry" he said confidently "I've already prepared for that. Here's what you'll do; I'll call her and ask her to give you an envelope containing one "document" or the other which you will bring to me, that way you can still meet me in the hotel, and we can both go together to get you a new phone. My wife won't even suspect a thing" he said confidently.

"Sir I'm very sorry but I'm no more comfortable with this idea, what if she finds out or someone sees me."

"You're sounding like a kid; how would she find out or do you plan on telling her that you'll be seeing me in the hotel?"

"No, not that I plan on telling her anything, but I don't understand why I have to meet you in the hotel to buy the phone."

"Don't you remember when I told you that if you want the phone then you have to do what I tell you?"

"Yes?" I answered interrogatively.

"Then if you're ready, you'll just do as I say and come see me tomorrow."

Trust me if you be an obedient daughter; the phone will be the first of many more things to come" he said forcing a smile up his face.

"Ok then, if you say so" I uttered in a low voice.

"I'm sure you know your way back, right?"

"Yeah" I said.

"It's alright then. You can go, I'll see you tomorrow. And please do not disappoint me."

"Ok but sir I don't have enough transport fare; I need some money to pay back home."

"Alright" Uncle Johnny said as he pulled out a lot of one thousand naira notes from his pocket and handed me three thousand naira.

"Thank you" I said visibly smiling, it was a lot more than my transport fare which was just two hundred naira.

"Expect more of that tomorrow" Uncle Johnny said as he opened the door for me to leave.

I left the hotel, boarded a taxi and in no distant time I was already at home. Luck was indeed on my side today as aunty Jean wasn't yet back from work.

I went straight to my room, pulled my clothes, and changed into something simpler. I was folding some of my outing clothes when I heard a knock on the door. Who could it be? my best guess was Tommy.

I opened the door and as expected Tommy was the one at the door.

"You can come in" I said. He walked into the room and sat on the plastic chair that I usually use for studying.

"What's up" I said trying to break the silence.

"I'm fine, you didn't attend lessons today?" he asked with his face looking blunt.

"Yea… I had to…"

"So where then did you go??" He asked sounding like a police officer.

I was in a state of dilemma, I was completely torn between two minds; a huge part of me wanted me to lie and save myself the stress of making him see reasons with me while a part of me wanted me to come clean and bear the consequences of whatever action he wanted to take.

Well, I ended up telling him everything! Tommy was dumbfounded but rather than complain or threaten me he began to develop trust in me. He felt that if I could tell him everything then that shows that I do not have any secret motive.

As he was still trying to recover from what I told him my phone rang and when I looked at the caller ID Uncle Johnny was boldly displayed on the screen.

"He is calling me" I told Tommy.

"Who is calling you?" he asked.

"Your dad."

I picked the phone call and turned on the loudspeaker.

"Hello, good evening, sir"

"Good evening my dear, how are you?" he asked.

"I'm fine, thank you sir."

"Are you done with your chores?" he asked.

"Yes sir"

"Hope you've been reading?"

"I'm trying" I began wondering why he was asking me such unusual questions.

"Is there anyone else with you in the room" he asked.

"No, I'm the only one."

"Are you sure" he questioned further.

"Yes sir, there's no one here with me."

"Okay, that's good. Elsie, do you know I've been missing you since you left. I can't stop thinking about you, you've been stuck in my head ever since." he said.

"I can't wait to see you tomorrow."

"Yeah, me too" I responded.

"Hope you won't disappoint me tomorrow??" He asked.

"I won't."

"I know you know what I mean, I hope you won't disappoint me" he asked once again.

"I won't disappoint you" I said trying to sound convincing.

"I hope so, I want to have some rest, please take good care of yourself. I'll see you tomorrow. Goodnight, dear, I love you" he said.

That last sentence changed Tommy's mood; he instantly became restless.

"Aren't you going to respond to me" Uncle Johnny asked sounding hurt.

"I love you too, goodnight" I said and hung up immediately.

My statement must have added salt to injury as Tommy kept pacing up and down the room.

"Did you just tell my dad that you love him??" He fired.

"In my presence??"

"I just needed to say that so that I can end the call" I said sheepishly.

"Is that why you told him that you won't disappoint him, or are you hoping to sleep with him??"

"No, God forbid!"

"I just want him to get the phone for me then after that everything will be over."

"So, you want to give him your body just because of a phone? Why can't you just ask my mom she'll get it for you" Tommy said visibly angered.

"Your mom has done a lot for me already; it would sound very ungrateful going to ask her for a phone. Besides I never asked her before she did all the things, she did for me. I know what I am doing; there's no need to be worried" I said.

"So that's the flimsy excuse you want to give, I should have just told my mom everything the day she met me in your room" Tommy said as he stumbled out of my room banging the door on his way out.

The following morning, there were very few clouds in the sky and the sun radiated it's heat energy. It was the perfect weather for doing the laundry.

As I washed my clothes, I could only imagine the events that would unfold today. If that man is hoping to have sex with me then he has failed because I can't lose my virginity to someone as old as he is. No!! I can't do that.

I was brought back to reality when Bobby, my aunt's youngest son came to call me.

"Elsie, my mommy is calling you" he said and ran back inside.

I washed my hands, got up and went to meet my aunt.

"Yes ma, you sent for me."

"I need you to give this envelope to your uncle, he said he's at the junction. He sounded very urgent, so you must be fast and please be very careful with it, ok?"

"Yes ma" I replied.

She then gave me the sum of $40 to pay for my fare. I rushed into my room and changed into a better-looking gown, packed my hair, and rubbed a little powder.

In less than five minutes I was on my way, I stopped in front of the hotel which was actually very far from the junction.

Uncle Johnny must have it all planned because he knew very well how far junction was from the hotel; so, he told my aunt won't get suspicious when I stay for a long while.

As I entered the elevator a lot of voices kept speaking in my head. What if he succeeds in corrupting me, what if he rapes me? What if this turns out to be the first of many extra marital affairs with my uncle.

I kept pondering upon my thoughts until I got to the front of room 406. It wasn't too late; I still had the chance to turn back and go home.

I wanted to leave the hotel, I wanted to go back immediately. My spirit was willing, but my flesh was weak, and my flesh overpowered my spirit. I knocked softly on the door, and Uncle Johnny opened…

Chapter 10

So Unfaithful

I couldn't believe it! Tears strolled down my cheeks as I looked from the pew at the back where I sat.

Their hands were cupped in each other as they walked down the aisle. My sight was blurry so I couldn't identify the lady in the wedding gown.

They had gotten to the pulpit and were now looking into each other's eyes.

"Do you Johnny take this woman to be your lawfully wedded wife, to live together in matrimony, to love her, comfort her, honor and keep her, in sickness and in health, in sorrow and in joy, to have and to hold from this day forward, as long as you both shall live?"

"Ye…"I was woken up by the beeping of my alarm sound.

Phew! I had been dreaming all along.

But why would Johnny want to get married to another woman? Is there any way I have failed as a wife? I asked myself.

Despite my busy schedule I've always being trying my best to manage the home, I even brought in my niece to live with us to cover for my shortcomings. So, what could that dream signify? I had no answers, the only thing to do was to go to God in prayer. I said a short prayer and I with faith I believed that everything was settled.

I looked out my window, it was bright already; the golden rays of the sun gave a bright coloring to the clouds and meadows. The weather was exceedingly bright; a lovely way to kickstart a Saturday. I turned over and faced the other side of the bed; it was empty. Femi wasn't around because of the project he said he was carrying out. I sat upright on my bed, stretched a little and finally managed to get up.

I really found it hard concentrating on whatever thing I was doing. Any slight event that happened kept giving me a flashback of the dream I had earlier this morning.

Over time I suspected that Johnny was cheating on me. Since he started sleeping outside the home in front of one conference, or one business meeting or the other. Especially when he began to deny me sex.

A lot of events took place that made me very suspicious. I suspected that he was having extramarital affairs especially with one of his students who just graduated from the University where he worked. Her name was Sonia Enola.

You may be wondering how I got to know her, well I had received a lot of reports from friends that my husband was always posting pictures of her and sometimes both together on his WhatsApp status.

I had never seen it first-hand, so I decided to not jump into conclusions. It appeared Johnny had restricted me from viewing his status and that made me more suspicious.

But what struck me the most was when I saw a fertility test result, he carried out with the so-called Sonia in his drawer. Surprise was an understatement for what I felt.

Why would my husband take his student to the hospital for a pregnancy test. Were they planning on having a baby or what? I needed answers, I needed to speak with my husband.

When Johnny finally came back home from another "academic function." I made up my mind to get to the root of whatever was going on. As soon as he entered the room, I held the test results in the air for him to see. Once he recognized it, his countenance changed. Fear gripped him and he was overwhelmed with shock. He tried to act normal and pretended like he wasn't surprised.

"Jean what are you doing with that paper?"

"Johnny, you went to run a pregnancy test with your student! Who is she?"

He kept quiet like a mouse as if thinking of what next to say.

"Johnny who is Sonia??"

"I don't understand why you would be asking such baseless questions. How many times do I have to tell you that Sonia is one of the brightest students in my department and because of that I naturally became close to her."

"Is that enough reason to follow her to carry out a pregnancy test??"

"Of course, yes; it is enough reason. She wanted to run a pregnancy test, so I decided to accompany her to quicken the process."

"Hmm… I hope so."

I said trying to convince myself into believing him. Despite his excuses I wrote down her full name and even went further to search for her on Facebook. I got to discover that she had two Facebook accounts; one of which the last postdated to about eight years ago while the other appeared to be her current functional account. Maybe she had lost access to it.

As I scrolled through her timeline I couldn't even figure anything special about her that would make my husband attracted to her. I even saw a picture of her where she was pregnant.

So, my suspicion immediately proved momentary like a fly that only lives for a day. I dismissed the thought of Johnny cheating on me but the dream I had still recreated my fears and sent chills down my spine.

Although I wasn't certain if my husband was cheating on me, I always prayed that God would help him to remain faithful.

In the middle of thoughts, a phone call came tearing the quietness and serenity of the environment. Johnny was the one calling, I can say without exaggeration that I had called him more than five times the previous night; none of which he picked.

"Hello" I said in a downcast tone.

"Honey good morning" he replied.

"Morning, I've being calling since last night, but you didn't respond to my calls nor my WhatsApp messages."

"My dear I'm very sorry, I've been busy ever since. No spare time to even do anything, it's been work all through."

"Okay then… It's alright"

"Yeah, even now that I'm calling it's regarding the project. I need a very important document as soon as possible, I forgot to take it with me when I was leaving. So, I don't really know but the only way out here is for someone; maybe Elsie, to bring it to me."

"Which document are you referring to?" I asked.

"It's in my briefcase, it's already packaged in an envelope. So, you'll just send Elsie to bring it to me at junction."

"Alright" I answered.

"But I'll have to send your son Elsie is busy with some chores" I said.

"Jean… Just send her! I'm waiting. She'll be more careful and cautious with it. And tell her to hurry up, I need it urgently!" Johnny said as he abruptly ended the call.

I called Elsie, gave her the envelope containing the documents and instructed her on what to do.

But as soon as she left, I began to feel weird on the inside, a strange feeling encompassed me. I started feeling like something was not right somewhere…

As Elsie left the house, I knew very well where she was going to. I had not spoken to her since last night and I don't know what she has in mind to do.

I thought telling my mom what was going on behind her back? But it could be that Elsie had a plan, she can decide not to go to the hotel or even refused entering the room.

There are many ways she can avoid seeing my dad. I decided to wait, if she stays for too long then I'll uncover the truth in the open.

Elsie knocked softly on the door and Uncle Johnny opened. He smiled as soon he saw her in a somewhat diabolical looking manner.

"I'd almost concluded that you won't be coming anymore."

"Did my wife ask you anything?" He inquired.

"No, why would she?" I asked verbally.

"Ok that's good, now let's get to the business of the day. First of I need you to massage my back like you usually do. Just open the first drawer, you'll see the oil lotion. That's what you'll use" Femi said as he lay face down on the bed almost unclad with only a pair of boxers.

Sluggishly, I brought out the oil lotion. As I got to the bed, I noticed goosebumps all over his back. Which signified that he was desperately anticipating my touch.

I massaged and massaged and massaged; then after he felt he was satisfied; Uncle Femi finally spoke.

"It's not only my back you'll massage today. You'll also massage that area, I'm sure you know what I'm saying" he said smiling.

"Which area do you mean?" I asked.

"Sir I'm here because of the phone you promised me."

"Elsie" Uncle Johnny said sitting upright.

"The phone is not a problem, let's just do this thing quickly."

"Sir I don't know what you're talking about" I said pretending to be naive.

"Habba! Nawa for you . Let me touch you, I want to feel you, I want to spank your bum and bite your tip.

His hands were now on my laps, and he had
slowly started moving them upwards.

"Sir I can't do that o, you're my aunt's husband!!"

"And so? No one would know about it" he said letting out a seductive smile.

"Sir I can't, it's not right."

"Didn't you know that before you came here, it's now that you're here that you want to turn me down.

See, I need you now more than ever, my heart yearns for you like the deer yearns for water. I know you're scared probably because you're a Virgen but you have to trust me. I'll go very easy on you. Afterwards, you'll even begin to enjoy it" he said_trying to convince me.

"Even if, I can't have sex with you. It's not right."

"Look I'm ready to buy you the phone and any other thing you want, just accept my humble request.

I love you; I love you so much and that's why I want us to do this."

"Sir I can't! I can't! I'm sorry but I can't!"

He wasn't relenting, he must have used all the tricks in the box as frustration filled his face.

But just when I thought he had given up; the devil in him rose like a flood. Uncle Femi started putting his hands under my gown. He tried raising my gown up, but I withstood him.

His hands were now concentrated on my bobs in what had now turned out to be a struggle.

"Sir please, stop this! It's not right. Ahh... you're hurting me."

It seemed like my words became deaf to him; his hands had unhooked my bra from within my gown. He used one of his hands to restrain me while the other was foundling my bobs.

While I screamed in pains, Uncle Johnny moaned in immense pleasure.

"Is this how I'm going to lose my virginity?" I asked myself.

I'm I really going to get raped by my uncle due to my stupidity. Is this really going to be the end?

Chapter 11

Meeting in Secret

It has been more than two hours since Elsie left the house, I began getting worried. My mom too was beginning to ask questions as to why Elsie wasn't back yet.

I was becoming more and more troubled. A second couldn't go by without me glancing at the time.

"Tommy, please ask Elsie to come and see me; I need her assistance" my mom said.

"She's still not back."

"The junction isn't that far; she should be back by now. Let it not be that she has lost her way, please get me my phone; so, I can call my husband. I need to make sure he has received the document and I hope Elsie is alright."

I was eager to let the cat out of the bag, but I didn't allow my nerves to get the best of me. I handed my mom her phone and hung around so that I could listen to her conversation with my dad.

She dialed his number; I could hear the ringing, but my dad didn't pick. She called him again; but unfortunately for us there was still no response.

"Why is Johnny not taking my calls, I hope all is well ."

She was about dropping her phone when she decided to try Elsie's line.

I could hear the beeping of the phone call from where I stood. Just like my dad, she didn't pick up.

Now my mom was beginning to get anxious, she called her two more times but to no service. That was when she started getting paranoid.

"Why aren't they answering my calls? They're getting me worried., What could be the issue?" She asked herself.

"Tommy, you'll help me call them with your phone; I don't know why they're not responding to my calls."

I wasn't surprised that they weren't picking up and I knew trying their lines with my phone was just a waste of time.

I just wanted to tell mom everything, I wanted to let her know that my dad had been trying to lure the girl who she brought to live with us into having sex with him. I wanted to let her know that things were not as it seems. I wanted to let her know that both my dad and Elsie could be on the hotel bed right now!

But when I thought of what the outcome may be, I resolved to looking for another means to handle the issue. If my mom eventually finds out... I doubt if anything could make her remain married to my dad.

They'll go their separate ways. We will be brought up by a single parent is not something I'll want myself let alone my younger ones to experience. I canremember one of our neighbor's sons who's currently in the police station awaiting trial. He was a boy with a very promising future, Benjamin was self-disciplined, obedient, and very respectful, he was a very close friend of mine. But when his parents got divorced, his life changed for the worse. After the divorce, only him and his dad lived together.

Benjamin's dad was a very busy man. He will leave very early in the morning and come back very late from work. There was no guardian to correct and control his excesses. He began keeping bad friends, started moving with the boys on the street and slowly he started turning into a nuisance.

It didn't take long for him to get initiated into one of the dominant cult groups in the area. Ben went on to start drinking, smoking, doing drugs and causing chaos in the neighborhood.

At that time my parents strictly warned me to dissociate myself from him because he was no longer who he used to be.

Sooner than expected; his dad got to know about what his son had turned into, but it was too late, the fine grape had already gone sour.

Anyone passing by their house that day could hear Benjamin's father at the top of his voice seriously scolding his son. Meanwhile Benjamin kept quiet all through, one would have thought that Benjamin must have heeded to his dad's advice.

But as his dad came back from work the next day, everything that belonged to his son was gone. He was totally devastated. His only son had run away from home to live a life without experience, knowledge, or guidance.

Last we heard of Benjamin was that he and some other boys got arrested after they were caught with hard drugs.

With all those happening, I wouldn't want to rush into a decision that could change my life forever. I decided to not say anything because when the truth will reveal itself when it is ripe.

My struggle with Uncle Johnny was now increased, he had successfully opened my zip and held me down, but I didn't give up. Johnny was all over my body, twisting my tips, squeezing my cheeks, and trying to reach my thing. He kept moving back and forth but I didn't allow him to go any further.

Luck then shone on me when his phone rang.

It was Aunt Jean, he ignored it, but it rang once more; Still, he didn't pick. After a while my phone also rang, the calls made him angry, so he took both phones, put them on silent and stretched his hand to drop them on the sofa.

This was my chance, I noticed that the toilet door wasn't locked; I could quickly enter inside and save myself from anything that would happen.

I made a move for it, as soon as I tried moving, just like a flash Uncle Johnny immediately got hold of me and pulled me back to the bed. There was no hope for me, this was surely going to be the end for me.

I tried hitting and slapping him, but it was all useless, I then resolved to shouting still Uncle Johnny closed my mouth with his hand.

The fight continued for a while, but it didn't take long for him to overpower me. He got hold of my both hands and put them behind me, he raised my gown up and the only obstruction left was my panties.

Jackpot! The smile on his face at that point was like someone who finally won the lottery after playing for a huge number of times.

I was all in tears, there was nothing I could do; I had used up all my energy in shouting and struggling with him. He looked at my pathetic face, but he didn't give a rat's ass.

Slowly he carefully shifted my panties to the side like a kid opening a birthday present.

We had gotten to the climax of the occasion. There was nothing hindering him anymore, he reached for his boxer and wanted to bring out his JT…

I didn't give up; I gathered the last strength in me and screamed as loud as I could.

"What is wrong with you? Do you want to get me into trouble??" He shouted terribly annoyed.

"Sir this is rape, you're forcefully trying to have sex with me, and you expect to keep quiet" I said almost in tears.

"Knock, knock" someone was at the door.

Alas! my savior had come. Whoever it was, he must have been attracted by my shriek.

"Do you see what you have caused" Johnny thundered with rage in his eyes.

"You better remain quiet and don't do anything stupid" he said.

Johnny went to the door and opened to see who it was.

"Good day sir" it was one of the hotels attendants.

"Good day" Uncle Johnny replied.

He only opened the door a little and blocked the entrance so that no one could see inside.

"Sir we received a noise complaint about your room, someone reported that he's been hearing screams from this room, we hope everything is fine?"

"Of course, everything is fine" Uncle Johnny said faking a laugh.

"I was actually laughing because of the movie I was watching, whoever reported must have misjudged the sound; everything is okay" Johnny said sounding innocent.

I listened to them, and I could only wish that whoever was at the door would just push the door open. That was the moment reality dawned on me, it was a golden opportunity to finally save myself.

The toilet door was open, Uncle Johnny was at the door, nothing was stopping me now. I tried to get up, but I was seriously weakened, there was no strength left in me.

But I needed to go now; it was either now or never. I mustered every single energy left in me and crawled down to the toilet door. I pushed it open, entered inside and locked the door behind me.

As soon as I locked the door, Johnny was done speaking with the man; he must have successfully convinced him with his sweet words; into thinking nothing was going on.

He quickly locked the door and hoped to continue from where he stopped, I was able to see him through the toilet door, he looked at the bed, but I wasn't there. He immediately became terrified.

"Elsie!" He called, but I didn't answer.

"Elsie! please come out, don't worry I won't try to do anything with you again, please just come out from wherever you are."

"YOU ARE WICKED, YOU ARE A VERY WICKED MAN" I said in tears.

I sat on the floor and rested my back on the door.

"Please, I'm very sorry" he said.

"I never thought it would turn out this way."

"You are heartless, you are a very heartless" I said audibly crying.

I didn't care whatever he had to say but I was ready to remain in this toilet for as forever...

Chapter 12

Unfaithful Wives Regions

Given the fact people are not exactly honest when talking about adultery, finding the places with most unfaithful wives sounds almost impossible. Still, I managed to select cities, where women are, apparently, most likely to cheat.

First, let's focus on what types of marriages or relationships exist, to understand what adultery is considered for in different parts of the world and whether it all comes down to the same, a partner's lost trust.

So, nowadays, we have monogamous societies, where a state of being married to one person at a time is practiced, and polygamous societies, where having more than one partner is a norm. Moreover, even within polygamy, we can make a difference between polygyny, which implies a marriage between a man and several women, whereas, in the case of polyandry, it's the opposite.

Also, there are group marriages, where multiple wives and multiple husbands which are, in fact, the family unit.

While polygamy is banned in several developed countries, it seems like serial polygamy, "is generally accepted practice" as we witness it daily, having people divorced and then marring with someone else all the time.

Unfortunately, in the US only, 67% of the second marriages and even 73% of the third, end in divorce. So, the conclusion would be that polygamy exists in every society but in different forms.

Furthermore, these statistics don't surprise if we consider how common is cheating in this country. The percent of Americans who admitted they've been cheating ranged between 20% to 25% for men compared to 10% and 15% for women in the period between 1991 and 2008, that's more than a decade ago, and those are just the ones being honest about it.

In addition, according to Ashley Madison, "the global leader for affairs," Seattle, Denver and Dallas are the cities with most unfaithful husbands in the country, while San Antonio cheaters are not far behind.

When ranking cheaters by state, it seems like Texas cheaters lead the way, since out of 20 top cities with the most unfaithful men, five are in Texas. So, those hubbies cheating in Dallas are just the top of an iceberg. However, those Boston's cheating spouses should know that adultery is still considered as a criminal offense in Massachusetts, more precisely, a crime against chastity.

The opinions on whether monogamy is "natural" or not for human species are rather interesting. In a book called "The Myth of Monogamy," Professor David Barash, a zoologist and professor of Psychology Emeritus at the University of Washington, and intriguingly his wife, Judith Eve Lipton, M.D., also a psychiatrist, who are married for more than 35 years argued that we are carrying the "biological imprint of polygamy," while discussing monogamy within the animal kingdom.

Even though they didn't justify infidelity among people, aiming to bust the myth of monogamy, they suggested "cheating is the rule," for both sexes, for almost every species. So, when it comes to mammals, there are only a very few species living in, what might be called "monogamous arrangements," or less than 5% of around 5,000 species.

Besides otters, some bats, foxes and occasionally wolves, we, humans, engage in monogamous relationships as well. The question is, why we defy biology by practicing monogamy?

To answer this question, let's turn to a timeline of major events in the history of human society and the evolution of sexual behavior. Starting from the dawn of man, it's almost impossible to give an answer to questions like "were cavemen monogamous?".

However, several ethnographic descriptions of hunter-gatherer societies as well as work of anthropologists during the last two centuries like Lewis H. Morgan and Friedrich Engels as well as geographer Jared Diamond, propose that prehistoric societies were built on the foundations of equality and polyamory, where anyone of any gender can have more than one partner.

After all, in societies where a community was a vital factor of one's survival, sharing was of utmost importance.

Fast forward some 15 000 years in the future, we are living in a world where both polygamy and monogamy are practiced. The agricultural revolution which had happened a few millennia ago brought with itself a shift from matrilocal to patrilocal residency.

In plain English, this shift implies that a man is to remain living in his father's house after reaching maturity and bringing his wives to live there as well. Moreover, there are some suggestions that partner availability, or to be more precise partner scarcity may have played an important role in the evolution of monogamy.

In addition, STDs also might have played a role in establishing this mating behavior, since larger societies were more prone to suffer from STD epidemics. At the end, we can't diminish the influence of religion on sexual behavior. Christianity and monogamy go hand in hand, the same as Islam and polygyny.

Even in countries which are embodiments of Western civilization, like Canada, polygamy is still happening in some Muslim communities, while a Muslim polygamy matchmaking apps are a real thing.

So, to wrap up. The human being and its behavior, including sexual, can't be observed from the biological aspect only. Therefore, it's heavily influenced by the culture it belongs, while race doesn't directly have that important role. The famous anthropologist Edvard Taylor once wrote that culture is that "complex whole which includes knowledge, belief, art, law, morals, custom, and any other capabilities and habits acquired by man as a member of society."

That way when thinking about cheating and unfaithfulness, it's important to determine what countries, societies, and cultures are we are taking into consideration. Therefore, determining the most unfaithful race it's not exactly something traceable.

What counts as "cheating"? And more importantly for our today's list, why women cheat?

The term is vague, and it goes from being sexual to being even or "only" emotionally unfaithful to your partner, and once again it depends on where the one comes from. The reason why someone cheats, is, on the other hand, heavily impacted by the person's sex.

While there are some overlaps, the reasons men cheat is more of a "physical" nature, comparing to women, were psychology beats biology. Their disloyalty is often triggered by a lack of intimacy, loneliness, high expectations, and by a feeling of negligence and underappreciation.

Nowadays, to find some attention, women and man often end up on social media, making the Facebook one of the top "places" where do most affairs happen or at least began. Once they hit the road, the places cheaters go are usually coffee shops, restaurants, bars, etc.

For our research on the world's cities with most unfaithful wives, the idea was to restrict to those women cheating in marriage, and therefore break the marriage contract by getting a divorce.

Since data for each city can't be traceable, first, we focused on countries. We breezed through some divorce rate statistics worldwide, using extensive OECD's report, and a few other articles, such as Futurity's article on divorce in African countries and a report on Australia's divorce rates, only to single out those with the highest divorce rates.

Speaking of Australia, according to our research on countries with most faithful husbands, Aussies are the world's most loyal hubbies. For today's list, we've also consulted our articles on countries with most unfaithful wives and countries that cheat the most in the world.

Once we got a grip on countries where wife's adultery is most possible we also checked for the level of happiness in these countries as well as how sexually active are its citizens.

After all, those unhappiest countries with high sexual activity are probably those where people cheat more, right? After narrowing it down to 25 countries where the women and man are likely to cheat more, we put in use Quora and Reddit, in order to find out which are the cities with most unfaithful wives in those countries.

Chapter 13

Women Ending Marriages

The Betrayed Husband

Like most men, you probably didn't see your wife's affair coming, not only because your wife may not have seemed all that interested in sex; but also, because you have the belief that your wife is a "good girl."

Unfortunately, up until very recently, men were regularly divorced by their wives without ever knowing about their wives' affairs and infidelities.

Woman in a Limbo

Like most women, prior to cheating on your husband, you always proclaimed yourself to be "not the type" who would ever cheat. However, also like most women, AFTER they've cheated, you're probably shocked and disturbed by your behavior, but at the same time. You can't stop cheating or let go of the idea of a new relationship.

Find Out the Real Reasons Women Divorce

There is a Specific Pattern Women Follow Before Divorcing Their Husbands.

Like most men, you probably didn't see your wife's affair coming, not only because your wife may not have seemed all that interested in sex; but also, because you have the belief that your wife is a "good girl." Unfortunately, up until very recently, men were regularly divorced by their wives without ever knowing about their wives' affairs and infidelities.

Like most women, prior to cheating on your husband, you always proclaimed yourself to be "not the type" who would ever cheat. However, also like most women, after they've cheated, you're probably shocked and disturbed by your behavior; but at the same time, you can't stop cheating or let go of the idea of a new relationship.

Women's marriages have been following the same pattern which is described in detail below for a long time, and they will continue to follow the same predictable pattern unless we develop and accurate understanding of females, particularly regarding sexuality.

Unfortunately, society's preoccupation with male infidelity and male commitment issues has and continues to keep a light from being shined too closely on female infidelity and female commitment issues.

The media has finally begun to acknowledge, although to a small degree, the widespread problem of female infidelity. But to be clear, female infidelity is one of the most prevalent problems that couples are facing today in their relationships.

When people write and speak about why women cheat, they often regurgitate outdated information or intentionally leave out basic information — because it's not politically correct to talk about women's true sexual nature.

However, without these missing pieces of information, it's impossible to understand, and to subsequently fix, many of the real problems couples are facing today in their relationships.

Currently, Women Are Initiating 75% Of All Divorces

The Four "Stages" Women Often Move Through During the Course Of Their Long Term Relationships

It was discovered that what it was experiencing was quite normal. In fact, women are the most likely to divorce in their late twenties and thirties after an average of 4 years of marriage. During this time, it's quite common for women to experience a pre-midlife crisis, which is like the male midlife crisis, only with an important difference - a difference that can make women more likely to cheat than men.

Over time, many women begin to lose interest in sex. It is not uncommon for them to spend a great deal of energy trying to avoid physical contact with their husbands because they fear it might lead to a sexual encounter. They frequently complain of physical ailments to avoid having sex and often try to avoid going to bed at the same time as their husbands.

They view sex as a job, not unlike doing the dishes or going to the grocery store. Some women in Stage 1 claim they feel violated when their husbands touch them. Their bodies freeze up and they feel tightness in their chest and/or a sick feeling in their stomach. Most women in Stage 1 feel as though there is something wrong with them, that they are in some way defective. They are also fearful that their disinterest in sex will cause their husbands to cheat, or worse yet, leave them.

Women experience reawakened desire stimulated by an encounter outside the marital relationship. Whether these encounters with a "new" man involves sex or remain platonic, women will typically give a tremendous amount of emotional significance to these encounters.

Many women haven't felt any sexual desire for a long time. Many experiences tremendous guilt and regret, regardless of whether their new relationships are sexual, merely emotional, or both.

Most begin to experience what could be termed an identity crisis - even those who try to put the experience behind them. Constant reminders are everywhere. They feel guilt when the topic of infidelity arises, whether in the media, in conversations with family and friends, or at home with their husbands.

Women can no longer express their prior disdain for infidelity without feeling like a hypocrite. They feel as though they have lost a part of themselves. Reflecting society's belief that women are either "good" or "bad," women will question their "good girl" status and feel that they might not be deserving of their husbands.

Many will try to overcome feelings of guilt by becoming more attentive toward and appreciative of their husbands. However, over time many women will move from appreciation to justification.

To justify their continued desire for other men, women will begin to attribute these desires to needs that are not being met in their marriage, or to their husband's past behavior. Many women will become negative and sarcastic when speaking of their husbands and their marriages and it is not uncommon for an extramarital affair to follow.

Like most men, you probably didn't see your wife's affair coming, not only because your wife may not have seemed all that interested in sex; but also, because you have the belief that your wife is a "good girl." Unfortunately, up until very recently, men were regularly divorced by their wives without ever knowing about their wives' affairs and infidelities.

Woman in a Limbo

Like most women, prior to cheating on your husband, you always proclaimed yourself to be "not the type" who would ever cheat. However, also like most women, after they've cheated, you're probably shocked and disturbed by your behavior; but at the same time, you can't stop cheating or let go of the idea of a new relationship.

Unfortunately, society's preoccupation with male infidelity and male commitment issues has and continues to keep a light from being shined too closely on female infidelity and female commitment issues.

The media has finally begun to acknowledge, although to a small degree, the widespread problem of female infidelity. But to be clear, female infidelity is one of the most prevalent problems that couples are facing today in their relationships.

When people write and speak about why women cheat, they often regurgitate outdated information or intentionally leave out basic information — because it's not politically correct to talk about women's true sexual nature.

However, without these missing pieces of information, it's impossible to understand, and to subsequently fix, many of the real problems couples are facing today in their relationships.

Chapter 14

The Marriage

Gloria's marriage to powerful Italian businessman Angelo DiSalvo was an empty sham, and she was determined to get a divorce. But Angelo didn't want one. In the circumstances, Gloria found that totally unbelievable. Why would he want to hang on to a wife he'd been blackmailed into marrying!

Gloria's lonely wedding night had set the pattern for the past five years, but now she couldn't sleep for wondering what motivated her husband. Why, suddenly, was he making advances to her when he had ignored her for so long?

With a fleeing glance over her shoulder, Gloria hurried down the steps and into the wine bar. It was dark and crowded with lunchtime drinkers. She couldn't see Paul. She wasn't tall enough to see past the clumps of business-suited men standing around.

A nervous tremor shot through her as she burrowed through the male clusters. She was so terrified of being seen, recognized. It was a relief to espy Paul's golden head in a far corner.

He stood up as she approached, tall, sophisticated, and very attractive, and her heart swelled with pride. 'You're late,' he complained.

'Sorry, I couldn't get away.' Short of breath, Gloria sat on to a seat and couldn't help spinning another glance around in fearful search of a familiar face.

'Stop that. You're on the wrong side of town to be seen.'

Gloria bent her blonde hair; her face was flushed and stiff. 'That man in the corner is staring at me!'

'Most men stare at beautiful women, and you are exquisitely beautiful, my love,' Paul murmured in a low, intimate tone, reaching for her slender hand. 'It gives me a real kick watching every male head turn when you walk by.'

'Does it?' Still unaccustomed to his compliments, Gloria looked up at him with a shy uncertainty that was oddly at variance with her designer suit. Her flawless face between the wings of her sleekly swept up blonde hair was captivated, her sapphire-blue eyes bright as the jewels in her ears.

'Why don't we go back to my apartment?' Paul ran a finger along her full lower lip and smiled smoothly as her skin heated.

Gloria stiffened. 'I can't. Not yet, you know how I feel,' she muttered in a stifled voice. Fear sprung up inside her as his handsome face turned hard and cold.

'And you know how I feel, Mrs. Julianne. I am frustrated if you must know!'

Gloria turned white. 'Paul, please...'

'For all I know, you're just playing a little game with me while your husband's out of town.'

Pain and distress filled her eyes. 'I love you...'

'Then when are you going to tell him you want a divorce?' Paul demanded.

If possible, Gloria got even paler, a hunted look tightening her exquisite features. 'Soon... I must pick the right moment.'

'Considering that on average he only sleeps one night a month under the same roof as you, I could still be sitting here this time next year. Maybe you're in love with the bastard.'

'How could I be?' She bent her head, her hands clenching tightly together. 'You know we don't have a normal marriage.'

'And it wouldn't the news as just love to get a load of that!' Paul sniggered.

'I don't think that's funny, Paul.'

'Well, the only thing that keeps me going is the knowledge that I may not be your lover, but he isn't either. You've got to admit that that's a real mystery. Look at you,' Paul mused. 'The virgin bride five years down the road and yet he's rarely seen in public without some beautiful bimbo clinging to his arm. Maybe he's gay.'

Her sensitive stomach curdled. She must have been mad to tell Paul the truth about her marriage. Not, of course, that he would do anything with it. She trusted him absolutely, but she was aware that she had been dangerously careless in her need to soothe his jealousy of Nico...

The very blood in her veins went cold when she faced up to what she still had ahead of her.

'Don't talk about him like that,' she urged tightly.

'You think the table is bugged? You're scared stiff of him, aren't you? I don't think you're ever going to pick up the courage to tell him you want your freedom. I think I'm wasting my time.'

'No...no, never,' Gloria whispered frantically, the thought of losing him filling her with panic. She just couldn't go back to what her life had been for the past five years. Empty, without focus, boring.

Before Paul, every day had stretched endlessly in front of her. She didn't have a social life. She didn't have friends. She was watched everywhere she went. The door of her prison had slammed shut on her wedding-day and she had been so dumb, so naïve, she hadn't even realized it until she'd tried to move beyond the bars.

'Then when?' he pressed moodily.

'Soon...I promise you.'

'I don't see why you can't just move out. It's not as though you don't have all the evidence you need to divorce him. Adultery is not about to go out of fashion with Nico Julianne around.'

'I must do it right, Paul. Don't you see that I owe him that?'

'I don't see that you owe him anything. In the eyes of the Church and the law, he's not even your husband,' Paul persisted.

Gloria glanced at her watch and spoken a breath of dismay. 'I have to go!'

Paul caught her by the shoulders and kissed her with practiced expertise. 'I'll phone,' he promised. 'Love you, darling.'

Gloria fled. It was three blocks to the fashionable hairdressers where she had been booked in for a long session of massage and beauty treatment. She took terrible risks to meet up with Paul and her head told her that the longer she put off asking Nico for a divorce, the more chance there was of her being found out. But then, what would it really matter?

Nico didn't care what she did. She saw him maybe once a month when he stopped over in New York, sometimes not even that over the past year. He might request that she play hostess for a business dinner, but of late even those requests had been few and far between. If he had to communicate with her, he did so through his staff.

In their entire marriage, Nico had never once taken her out in public. Not for dinner, not to the theater, not even party. Nico practiced his glittering social life with other women on his arm, never, his wife.

He slept in his own wing of the house and even that handful of nights a year that he stayed under the same roof, she had heard him go out late and return after dawn, so those nights didn't really count either.

For an instant, as she flew through the side-entrance of the hairdressers, she remembered when she had lain awake crying and listening for him. She was wondering in despair what was wrong with her, what she had done, what she had not done, what she could possibly do to make him notice her and acknowledge her existence.

Angrily she thrust the memory away. Time had taken care of that kind of nonsense. The child bride had grown up and wised up…

'I'm so sorry. I forgot my appointment,' Gloria murmured at the reception desk and as usual she insisted on paying anyway and she tipped as if there were no tomorrow.

The proprietor, Carlos, came up to her and offered to fit her in immediately but she sighed and said she was running late and sat down to wait for her chauffeur to draw up outside.

"Oh, by the way, Mrs. Julianne, " Carlos lowered his head, his beaded locks swinging colorfully." Your bodyguard called in with a message for you."

Gloria went rigid. She turned white as a ghost.

"Relax." His brown eyes met hers. "I told him you were in the massage-room."

Gloria turned red. "Thank you," she managed clumsily.

'' I'd better give you the message," he whispered. 'Mr. Julianne is waiting for you at home.'

Nico was what? Nico was waiting for her...Nico who had never waited for her once in five years? Nico was home when he wasn't due back in New York for another day.

Unwillingly, Gloria shivered, her stomach turning over sickly. For a split-second she was consumed by the sort of panic that made people jump out windows in a fire. Sheer cold terror.

Carlos sat down beside her; his hands planted on his knees. 'Baby, you're not cut out for this game you're playing'

'I don't know what you're'

'You've been coming here every week for five years. And the last couple of months what you've been feeling has been just blazing all over your face.' He sighed. 'But I don't want to go down in history as the idiot stupid enough to give Nico's wife an alibi. He's the kind of guy who probably breaks fingers. I get the shakes just thinking about it.'

Shame washed over her. 'I'm sorry.'

'And I'm sorry I can't be more help because it's been kind of nice seeing you happy for a change.'

'Mrs. Julianne...?'

Gloria flinched as her bodyguard, Bruce, cast a big, dark shadow over her. As she stood, he cast a suspicious, cold look at Carlos, who had been too physically close to his employer's wife for his liking.

As soon as the door slammed on the limousine, her composure collapsed. Carlos knew she was seeing someone. Dear God, she felt so humiliated. She also felt guilty as hell. Her hairdresser was afraid of being dragged into a marital affair.

Not that there was the slightest chance of that happening when Nico couldn't give two hoots what she did. But cheerful, joking Carlos, who had laughed her out of many a depression over the years, had been genuinely scared.

Everyone was afraid of Nico. Yet, she had never heard him shout. Early on in their marriage Gloria had walked in mortal terror of him until it had slowly sunk in on her, with the drip effect of his icy indifference, that she barely existed as a human being on his scale of importance.

He had married her to gain the shares her father had signed over to her. She had been part of a business deal, nothing more. Yet, there had been times at the beginning when she could have sworn that Nico looked at her with disguised disgust, when his voice could say the lightest things and sound like a stroke of naked threat, when his very presence in the same room had made her feel menaced.

That was when she had understood to hug the background, never draw attention to herself, avoid him whenever possible. She had assumed that he resented having had to marry her to get the shares. Yet divorce had always been within his reach. It was a mystery Gloria had yet to understand.

Now Nico, who had not varied his schedule in five long, endless years, had come home unexpectedly. That fact returned to haunt her, anxious though she had been to evade it. Her fingers clenched white-knuckled around her bag as she climbed the steps of the vast Georgian terraced house. The unfaithful wife, she thought painfully.

But she wasn't his wife, not his real wife, she reminded herself, just as she had often done in the weeks since she had met Paul. She should have demanded her freedom a long time ago. But her father would have been outraged and bitterly disappointed.

Gloria had spent the first seventeen years of her life pleasing her father, Mike, in every way she could. She had done as he advised five years ago. She had married Nico and it had been the biggest mistake of her life.

Nico had taken her freedom and given nothing in return, but that time was past, she reminded herself. It was almost two months since her father had died, the heart condition which had endangered his health for years having finally taken its toll.

'Mr. Julianne is waiting for you in the drawing-room,' Peter the butler informed her.

Gloria floated, nervous tension biting. As a rule, she didn't see Nico until he sat down at the dinner-table. The belief that something was wrong attacked her again.

He was standing by the marble fireplace, six feet two inches of overwhelmingly masculine male. Once she had looked at him and her heart had sung, her knees had weakened, and her voice had caught in her throat.

Now Gloria saw him always as if through a glass wall. Learning to detach herself had been lesson one...

Nico Julianne, the legendary Italian tycoon, possessor of fabled wealth and immense power. From his hand-stitched leather shoes to his fabulously tailored mohair-and-silk-blend pearl-grey suit, he was effortlessly elegant, supremely sophisticated. A man to die for, she had thought at seventeen, her impressionable little, teeny-bopper heart ready to burst with sheer excitement.

Nico was a devastatingly handsome male animal, quite stunningly gorgeous by any standards. Thick ebony hair, golden skin, riveting black eyes as dark as night. Wherever he went he was the focus of female attention. He knew it and was amused by it. He used it when it suited him.

Once, though she rarely allowed herself to recall it, Nico had focused that elemental aura of sexual energy on her.

Something had changed...something was different. Tension tapped in the air. Deep-set dark eyes scanned her. 'Your lipstick's smudged.'

Her fingers flew up to her mouth in a gesture of dismay. 'Is it?'

Winged ebony brows drew together in slight frown. Nico studied her intently. 'We haven't got much time, so I'll just move to the baseline. We're flying to Paris.'

Frozen with astonishment, Gloria echoed, 'Paris?'

Nico had already opened the door. 'Come on,' he said with unhidden impatience.

'You want me to go to Paris with you?' Gloria stressed helplessly. 'Now...like right now?'

'Yes.'

'But why?'

'A little business tied up with your father's estate.' Hooded dark eyes probed the amazement that flashed across her face.

Gloria was amazed. She amazed that there could be anything left to sort out concerning her father's estate. Although Nico had not even bothered to attend Mike's funeral, he had arrogantly assumed responsibility for instructing his lawyers to deal with her father's property and possessions.

While Gloria had been grieving, to bound up in her loss to consider the practicalities of death, everything her father owned had been sold, everything!

His beautiful house, his business investments, his very furniture, and personal effects had all been liquidated into cash at Nico's instruction. Gloria had not been left with a single memento. Her father, Mike Harrington, might never have existed for nothing remained to testify to his sixty-odd years on earth.

Gloria had been horrified by Nico's insensitivity but by the time she found out it had been too late for her to intervene. The deed had been done. As usual, Nico's orders had been carried out with speedy efficiency by his obedient staff.

A quiver of helpless antagonism ran through her. She lifted her silver head high. 'Something you actually overlooked?'

'No. Something, I was looking for has finally been located.' Harsh emphasis accompanied the assurance. An almost savage tension was briefly stamped in his hard, strong features as he read her mystified expression.

'At least I think it has been. For your own sake, pray that I am right,' he completed tightly.

Gloria stepped back from him, the chill, the sense of threat running along her every nerve-ending. 'For my sake? I don't know what you're talking about.'

'I hope not.' He swung on his heel.

Gloria headed for the stairs. A hard hand stayed her. 'Where do you think you're going?'

'To get changed.' Sudden fear licked at her. She stared in shock at the lean, powerful hand clamped to her slender forearm. Nico never touched her...never, not even in the most passing, casual gesture.

'There's no time for that. The jet's ready for take-off.'

'We will be coming back tonight?' Her voice rose an octave as he literally thrust her out of the house. 'I have nothing packed!'

'You'll manage.'

'What's going on?' Gloria demanded frantically as the limousine drew away from the curb.

Ignoring her with supreme despise, Nico picked up the phone and proceeded to talk at length in Italian.

She didn't understand a word. A fleeting recollection stirred. On their wedding-day she had told him she intended to learn his language. 'Don't waste your time,' he had mocked, and that had been the very first crack that appeared in her fantasy world.

Before the day was at an end, the crack had widened into a yawning gulf, but it had taken a lot longer for reality to banish that fantasy world she had wanted so badly.

Her temples throbbed with the tension in the air. Her inner turmoil did not show. She sat still, apparently composed, her manicured hands loosely resting on her lap.

In Nico's presence she had learned to conceal her emotions. Only that did not still the stormy flood of her hidden dismay and disbelief.

'What is this all about?' Gloria asked a second time.

Silence.

Stubbornly she persisted. 'I understood that Dad's estate was all settled.'

'Did you really? I wonder,' Nico responded quietly.

Something in his intonation disturbed her. Her delicate profile turned. She encountered eyes as dangerous as black ice. Her stomach muscles clenched, her skin chilling. She had a sense of approaching disaster so powerful that she felt briefly sick.

'If you would just explain what ?' she began.

'Why should I explain myself to you?' It was so clearly a growl of lancing derision that she was silenced.

'Young as you are, you are every man's secret fantasy...' Who would ever believe that those seductive words had been uttered by the husband who had ignored her very existence for five solid years? Yet, Nico had said those words the first day they met. Why had he lied? Why had he pretended? Had he wanted those shares in that shipping line that badly? He must have done.

It was patently obvious that she had never been Nico's secret fantasy. Bitterness tremored through her. Nico had used her without conscience, as had her father, who had gloried in Nico's wealth and status.

Pained by the response, Gloria looked blankly out of the window. She longed for Paul. Paul, who hadn't even known who she was when he'd first approached her, Paul, the very first man in her life to respond to her as an individual with feelings and needs and opinions of her own. He wanted only her. He wanted her for herself. He wasn't trying to use her.

In Paris, she would tell Nico that she wanted a divorce. There would be no more delay. She would not risk losing Paul. She was hungry to live a life of her own, hungry for the freedom which motioned so temptingly on the horizon.

Nico had stolen her youth, the teenage years when she should have been dating and having fun and loving. Why shouldn't she be greedy for what she had never had?

On the private jet she flicked through magazines, but her mouth curled several times as she watched the stewardess hover round Nico like some harem concubine, desperate to attract the sultan's favor.

A beautiful brunette had a bad dose of infatuation. Who better than Gloria to recognize the symptoms? After all, she had once been a victim herself. But now she was utterly detached from Nico and prided herself on the fact.

Nico, with his blazing Italian temperament and movie-star looks, didn't touch her on any physical or emotional level. He was unpredictable and ruthless. The cloak of civilization was thin.

He was also manipulative, arrogant, and vicious towards those who opposed or antagonized him. If she had been his real wife, she wouldn't have dared to sneak around with another man behind his back...

A limousine collected them at Charles de Gaulle Airport, carrying them through the heavy late afternoon traffic. The car drew up on a busy, crowded street. Gloria climbed out, too proud to ask yet again where they were going but looking around. Nico strode ahead of her into the nearest building. He was carrying an executive case. The building was a bank, she registered.

Three men were waiting in the foyer. One of them, whom she recognized as her father's solicitor, attempted to speak to her, but Nico cut him off very rudely. From below her lashes she stole a glance at her husband.

Dear God, but he was ignorant. In the wrong mood. Too frequently the only mood in which Gloria saw him. His manners were awful towards those unfortunates he considered to be lesser beings.

As one of them, Gloria felt a creature sympathy for the middle-aged man with his flushed, strained face.

A lift took them down to the vaults. The magical mystery tour, she reflected grimly. Were there more shares in that precious shipping line on offer? How could any man with Nico's fabulous wealth and assets be so disgustingly greedy? He had married her out of greed, hadn't he? Something for nothing. The shares had come free as her dowry.

The solicitor stuffed a key in her hand abruptly and then turned away.

"Give it to me,' Nico grated in a driven undertone, his simmering tension leaping out at her in an electrifying wave.

The key for a safety-deposit box, presumably belonging to her father, for why else would it have been put in her hand? She ignored him. For the very first time in their marriage, she ignored her husband, moving forward to watch the bank executive produce the box and leave it on the table before quietly leaving the small, bare room.

'Gloria...' Nico growled.

She refused to look at him. 'If it's my father's, it's mine...'

'Be very careful of what you claim.'

His savage warning pierced cold to the very center of her body. She looked at him and was paralyzed. Naked violence and aggression were engraved in his ferociously tense features. She hesitated and cast the key on the table by the box in sudden surrender.

'If it's in here you can relax,' Nico murmured between clenched white teeth. 'If it isn't, you'll be lucky to see the dawn break tomorrow.'

If what was in there? Perspiration broke on her short upper lip. Her legs suddenly felt weak and wobbly. Her sapphire-blue eyes clung to him in sick disbelief. But he wasn't looking at her. He was inserting the key in the box with a hand that wasn't quite steady.

She licked her dry lips. There was something more than shares at stake, something terrible enough to make even Nico threaten to come apart at the seams... She had never seen him close to the edge, never dreamed that he could lose control, but she was seeing it now.

The box was full of papers. With a burst of deep Italian, Nico began to search through them, discarding letters and photos which spilled in careless disarray across the table. He was pale and tense, his evident search becoming visibly more agitated.

Gloria focused on an envelope addressed to someone she had never heard of. She didn't even recognize the writing. Then she glimpsed a large, glossy photograph. In plain color, it described several men and women engaged in... In shock and disgust, Gloria avoided her eyes again. She started to tremble. Why had her father kept such an obscene thing in his possession?

'What is this stuff?' she whispered, since it was deliberately obvious that Nico knew far more about the contents of that box than she did. He had flicked past that photo without an ounce of reaction or surprise.

'What is it?' An edged laugh fell from his compressed mouth but there was no humor in the sound. 'It's a box of broken lives! Other people's secrets. Your father lived off his victims and their fear like some filthy cockroach!'

White as a sheet, Gloria gaped at him. 'How dare you talk about my father like that?'

Nico wasn't listening to her. He was still anxiously sorting through the papers. 'That he should leave me to clear up this filth is the final insult. I, Nico Julianne, reduced to soiling my hands because I cannot trust any other person alive with this obscene collection of human errors!

His trophies! He kept them to the last instead of destroying them! Cristo...the evil old bastard...'

Only the cold wall was supporting Gloria. She could not credit the crime that her late father was being accused of. Her mind was a complete blank over a furious sea of sick turmoil. 'What are you saying?' Her voice was so weak it was a thread of sound.

'Are you deaf?' Nico slung her a savage look of unconcealed loathing. 'Why do you think I married you? For your chocolate-box looks and your convent education?' he sneered. 'For your ability to act like a lady and fix stupid flower arrangements all over my house?'

'The shares,' she mumbled, shaking all over.

'There were no shares!' he raked back at her, the volume of his voice echoing off the walls with a rage that made her quail helplessly. 'There were never any shares. That shipping line didn't even exist!'

'You're lying,' Gloria framed through bloodless lips, barely able to stay upright.

Nico's attention was on the document he held in his hand. Suddenly, without any warning, he smashed his clenched fist down brutally hard on the tabletop. 'It's only a copy!'

'A c-copy of what?' As the table jumped, Gloria balked, plastering herself back against the wall, sick and dizzy.

'And this is the end of the trail...'

Nico prowled towards her like a tiger about to spring for her throat and drag her down. 'He gave the original to you, didn't he?' he murmured with lethal quietness, glittering black eyes settling on her with violent force. 'He gave it to you to keep safe...'

'G-gave what to me?' Gloria was so troubled she could barely speak. She couldn't think either.

'You know what I'm talking about. Not so innocent after all, it seems,' he breathed, backing her into a corner. 'If it isn't here, you have it. Mike was no fool. He knew I'd dump you like a hot potato if I got my hands on it. So, he gave it to you...so where is it?'

'Stop it!' Gloria gasped stricken, fearfully. 'Leave me alone!'

'If you don't tell me where that certificate is... you're in more danger now than you have ever been in your life,' Nico spelt out, waves of raw aggression splintering from his lowering stance a mere foot from her.

'I have lived with blackmail for five years to protect my family. I will not live with it one day longer!'

He had said the word, that terrifying word, and it danced about on the edges of the living nightmare she was being forced to endure. 'Blackmail'... It wasn't true, couldn't be true. Her father could not have been a blackmailer. On the edge of collapse, Gloria fought to stand her ground.

'I always wondered whether he intended it this way that you should be my life sentence,' Nico vented in a furious undertone. 'But I tell you now, I would sooner go to prison for putting my hands round that scrawny little throat and strangling the life force from your body. That would be the only life sentence I could live with!'

Terrified beyond endurance, Leah watched his dark, threatening face above hers black out and finally, mercifully vanish as she slid down the wall in a dead faint.

Chapter 15

The Obsession

Gloria recovered consciousness in the limousine. Nico was bending over her just as he had been doing before, she'd passed out. In one frantic movement she turned back from him and plastered herself up against the far door while she fumbled madly for the release mechanism, uncaring that they were during fast-moving traffic. 'Get away from me!' she screeched in panic.

'Fragile little creature, aren't you? A bundle of wild nerves suddenly.' Lounging back in a disturbing attitude of fluid relaxation, Nico examined her with unashamed satisfaction and a mocking smile, his aggression cloaked, his temper back under control. 'So where is that certificate?'

Her fingernails clenched painfully into her palms, etching purple crescents on the tender flesh. She needed that pain to be assured that Nico was still talking in the same nightmare fashion that he had been employing inside that suffocating little room. 'I've already told you that I don't know what you're talking about.'

'Well, if you didn't know you know now, and I want an answer.'

'I can't believe my father was a blackmailer.'

'Dirty, isn't it?' Nico treated her to a study empty of even the tiniest vein of compassion. 'But then he was a professional of the very highest quality. His field was the rich and famous and the skeletons he dug out of closets had to be juicy ones.

He was very good at what he did,' Nico drawled impassively. 'He never milked his victims totally dry. He never drove anyone to the point of trying to kill him. He made them pay for so long and then he let them off the hook, but he kept the evidence of their misdeeds to protect himself. He made a fortune...'

'I won't believe it!' Gloria tossed back shakily. 'I won't believe any of this!'

'Do you think he kept pornographic pictures in that box just for fun?'

Gloria's stomach curdled. She lowered her pounding head.

'Now if he took the trouble to retain a copy of the juicy skeleton, he trailed out of my family closet.' Nico's deep voice held a renewed edge of harshness. ' He also kept the original of the certificate, and since I have exhausted every other avenue, it is obvious to me that he must have given it to you.'

'He didn't give anything to me!' There was a tremble of hysteria in her tremulous response. She was in shock, deep shock, and in no state to combat his continuing pressure for her to produce something that she had not even known existed and certainly didn't have.

'You can't hold it over me. Just try and I will break you...'

'You're crazy!' she suddenly sobbed.

'This far, I have been remarkably kind and patient. I have been on a leash for five years,' Nico grated in an embittered undertone. 'I was only safe if I stayed married to you. I thought you might run home to Daddy. You never did, and one thing did become clear to me, horrifically clear over the years. You are in love with me.'

'What?' Gloria interrupted shakily.

'You are obsessed with me. Do you think I don't know this?' Nico sent her a shimmering look of contempt. 'Any normal woman would have left me by now and given up all hope of having her love returned... but not you! You stayed the course, loyal to the bitter end, obscenely faithful and well-behaved, giving me no excuse to complain of the devil's bargain I made!'

'Faithful'? Hysteria was tearing at her convulsing throat. Dear heaven, he believed what he was saying! Nico believed that she loved him. He thought she had stayed because she loved him. Paul's name floated on the very tip of her tongue, but sixth sense warned her not to muddy the waters further.

One thing at a time...only which? she wondered wildly. Life as she knew it had been shattered in the space of a few hours.

'I am not in love with you,' she murmured with as much dignity as she could contrive, her teeth gritting behind her peach-tinted lips. Absolute humiliation surrounded her as she appreciated that all along Nico had been thinking that his neglected, unwanted wife was just dying of love for him despite his complete indifference towards her. The ego he must have...the absolute, unashamed conceit.

'Listen, you're talking to the guy who was your seventeenth birthday present!' he slung back with savage derision.

'I beg your pardon?'

'Did you pick me out of some society magazine? Or did you see me in the flesh first? Did you take one look and rush to Daddy and say, "Daddy, this is the one I want!"?'

He was serious. He was serious. Her lower lip had parted company from the upper, a hectic pink firing her cheeks to dispel her previous pallor. 'You have to be out of your mind!'

'We are going to have this conversation. I have waited five years to stage it!' Nico asserted, skimming her with glittering dark eyes. 'All I know is that dear Mike did your dirty work for you. I was hunted down like an animal.'

'You are an animal...an insult to the species!' Gloria abruptly burst out. 'And your conceit is staggering!'

'Cristo...my perfect lady of a wife can actually raise her voice,' Nico drawled, surveying her with flaring dark eyes. 'You don't like the truth. It hurts your pride, but I know I was trapped quite deliberately.

I didn't even know who your father was that first time I came to the house. I was lured there by a third party, offering me a business proposition. Your father just so happened not to be available when I arrived, but you were. Romantically tending flowers in the conservatory, wearing something understated and white, literally armed to the teeth with virginal deceptions... I remember it so well.

'It wasn't like that!' she gasped in outrage.

'Any hot-blooded Italian would have looked twice and lingered,' Nico told her with scorn. 'And there you were, all shy smiles and blushes, eating me up with those big blue eyes as if you hadn't had a square meal in a week!'

'Stop it!' Gloria hissed, her voice breaking.

Nico studied her with uncompromising mockery, his beautiful mouth twisting. 'So, I was invited to dinner, and you played the piano like a concert pianist and sang like an angel.

Your every cultured virtue was paraded for my philistine benefit and somehow business never came into it. It might interest you to know, that I only had two questions I wanted answered that night but couldn't ask.'

'Really?' Gloria was staring blankly into space, every ounce of her remaining self-discipline directed at rescuing her shattered composure and combating the painful tidal wave of memories threatening to assail her. Two very different people...one encounter...such differing recollections of the same event.

'Were you over the age of consent? And did Daddy intend to protect you from the big bad world out there and sexual predators like me? Marriage was not, nor would it ever have been, on my mind.'

Nausea stirred inside her, and a bitter tide of mortification she could not withstand followed in its wake.

'Whose idea was it that I stay for dinner?'

Gloria froze.

'I thought so,' Nico breathed. 'Your idea. You told him you wanted me and that was that. He went digging and he dug up something that only two people alive knew about and neither of them would ever have talked about it!'

'What did he dig up?' she heard herself whisper helplessly.

'You know...Mike had plenty of warning that he was on borrowed time. He didn't go to his grave without passing that secret on to you,' Nico asserted softly.

'He passed nothing on to me...'

'And if you don't have it you have to know who has.'

The chauffeur opened the door beside her, and she almost fell out into the fresh air. She gazed down the quiet residential street in near panic.

She wanted to run. She knew where she was: Nico's Paris apartment where she had spent a quite unforgettable wedding night alone. He was unleashing everything on her at once, drowning her in a sea of shattering revelations, grinding her down with confusion, pain, and humiliation.

'Try it,' Nico said very quietly. 'Run and see what happens. I wouldn't let you get as far as the street corner.'

Trembling, pallid, Gloria entered the foyer in front of him and stepped into the lift.

'Memories...' Nico mocked, with a barbaric smile, as if he could see inside her.

Gloria knew she was still in shock. She said nothing. She also knew she wasn't up to the challenge.

Nico had been prepared. Nico had been waiting for this day, craving its arrival, longing for his revenge...just as he must have longed for her father's death to set him free from her.

'There are many functions I can perform to order but sharing a bed with you sadly wasn't one of them,' he delivered. 'He could make me marry you, but he couldn't follow me into the bedroom and force me to.'

'Shut up!' she screamed at him, the hysterical demand reverberating around the steel walls of the lift.

'So why did you never tell him that?' Nico persisted, going for the jugular when she was at her lowest decline with predictable calculation. 'Why didn't you ever tell him the truth about our marriage? Don't tell me that Mike wasn't desperate to hear the patter of tiny feet which would have made your position more secure!'

Her hands flew up to cover her convulsing face, a stinging flood of moisture dammed up behind her eyelids. 'Please...no more,' she whispered, and she didn't care that she was begging.

A pair of hands gripped her narrow shoulders. 'Ne...yes, you kept quiet about your pitifully empty marital bed all these years. Why?'

With a sudden superhuman effort which took him by surprise, Gloria tore herself free and fled across the hall of the huge penthouse apartment and down the bedroom corridor. She picked a room at the very end and vanished into the suite bolting the door behind her.

Slowly she slid down the back of the door and then she was forced to fly up again and cope with the shuddering spasms of sickness tearing at her abdomen. When it was over, she took off her clothes with the attitude of a sleepwalker and entered the shower cubicle.

My father, the blackmailer. She repeated the words to herself over and over as she sank down in a corner of the shower and let the water descend on her in sheets. She felt so dirty.

For the first time in her life, she felt dirty, and she didn't know what on earth she could possibly do to make herself feel clean again. Nico had torn the safe foundations of her very childhood from her.

Her mother, who had died when Gloria was four, was no more than a dim memory. The daughter of a minor English aristocrat, she had been cut off by her family for marrying Mike. Mike had never told his daughter why. He had never felt the need to explain himself.

Gloria's childhood had consisted of a procession of nannies followed by a succession of boarding-schools from an early age. Mike had travelled incessantly. Whenever she had pleaded with him to let her live with him, he had always had a ready excuse. She had reached adolescence before she finally appreciated that she was excess baggage in her father's life, and he was essentially a remote, self-contained, and cold man.

None the less she had always been aware that he cared about her as he cared about nobody else. He had been proud of her beauty, her education, her musical gifts. Those had all been saleable social commodities, she registered now. Mike had been ambitious for her.

He had wanted her to marry a man of wealth and position. He had always lived on the fringes of high society. He had been keen for his daughter to achieve a passport into that same society.

Gloria had grown up denied the warmth of family life but cocooned from harsh realities. Dependency had been bred into her bones, along with a desperate need to win her father's love and approval.

How could she ever have guessed that Mike was not a legitimate businessman? How could she ever have dreamed that her privileged upbringing had been financed by something so vile as the contents of that safety-deposit box? How could she have even begun to suspect that he had blackmailed Nico into marrying her?

Finally, she understood the cruel charade of her marriage, too late for her to do anything any differently. The five years had gone, couldn't be reclaimed either for her or for Nico. No wonder he despised her; no wonder he was so willing to believe that she knew the secret he had been prepared to go to extraordinary lengths to conceal. 'To protect my family', he'd said.

Ironically, she didn't want to know the source of the pressure put on him. He could keep that skeleton in the closet forever. In any case, Nico's family were strangers to her. He had a mother and three sisters whom she had never met.

She had often wondered whether they wondered about her and how Nico had explained so peculiar a marital relationship. But had he even bothered to explain? Like Mike, Nico was not in the habit of explaining himself unless he chose to do so.

How could he think she loved him? The ultimate humiliation. Not only a husband forced virtually at the point of a gun into marrying her, but a male convinced that even after five years of his painful neglect, indifference, and infidelity she still loved him! The wife from hell who would cling like a limpet through thick and thin.

Yet, as the water continued to beat down on her, Gloria slowly began to register a curious sense of growing inner strength which she had never felt before. She even managed to feel sorry for Nico.

He was afraid that she intended to try and employ her father's blackmail beyond the grave. Hence all the threats, the bullying, the intimidation. The news that she was in love with another man and couldn't wait to get a divorce would surely be blessing from heaven, a bolt of joyous blue across Nico's horizon!

She had wasted five years of her life, not one hour, not one day more would she sacrifice! Her father had once been her sole authority. She had allowed Nico to take over that role. Without any argument, she had tolerated Nico's behavior, even protected him sooner than let her father know that she had not been able to make a success of her marriage. Pride had done that, stupid pride.

She had been afraid, afraid of so much for so long. Afraid of leaving her safe cocoon of monied privilege to face the outside world. Afraid of her father's contempt and fury. Afraid that the truth about her marriage might literally kill her father with his weak heart. No more fear, she told herself now.

If Nico had been a victim, she had been too. At least she wasn't making as much noise about it as he was, she reflected grimly. His conceit still staggered her. Did he really think that that tender first love of a particularly naïve teenager had outlasted the first six months?

A loud knock sounded on the door.

'Open it!' Nico demanded roughly.

Mentally she blocked her ears. She had had enough of him for one day...enough of him forever. She tasted the concept and experienced a wave of positively heady relief. Nico did not possess a single virtue which appealed to her.

Five years ago, it had been an attraction of total opposites on her side. Sweet seventeen, choosing with her heart and her leaping pulses, not with her head.

'Gloria!' Nico raked with driven impatience.

He was not a male who respected her sex. He pursued one bimbo after another, brunette, redhead, and blonde. He didn't discriminate. They all had motorway-length legs, bounteous breasts, and big hair.

Gloria possessed none of those attributes and once that had been a source of torment to her, damaging an already weak self-image. She was worth so much more than. She had Paul to thank for that discovery. Paul had woken her up from her slough of inadequacy and passive acceptance. Paul had taught her to put herself first.

The way Nico did; the way Nico had always done. Nico had rejected and humiliated her from the outset of their marriage. What did she have to feel guilty about now? Hadn't she already paid for her father's sins? The payments in terms of her pain, loneliness and misery stopped now for all time, she swore to herself.

Standing up, switching off the shower, she was in the act of reaching for a towel when the door was suddenly struck with shocking force. The lock buckled and gave, the door slamming back on its hinges, framing Nico in the doorway. His lean, powerful body whipcord-taut, he glowered at her with eyes of flaming jet.

'Why did you lock yourself in here for?' he demanded ferociously.

Clutching her towel to her small, slender frame, Gloria was shattered by his violent intrusion, but she was also furious. 'Have you gone out of your mind?'

White teeth flashed against sun-bronzed skin; his narrowed gaze outraged. 'I was concerned for your welfare!'

Her welfare? Or her safety? Was that why he had kicked down the door like the Neanderthal he was? Had he been afraid that she planned to throw herself out the window? Of course, that might have been embarrassing for him.

Dealing him a veiled glance of disbelief, Leah stopped to gather up her discarded clothes.

'Your skin has the bloom of a camellia.'

Her lashes lifted slowly as she straightened. She blinked. Nico was staring at her in the most unbelievably disturbing way, his veiled gaze working intently over every exposed inch of flesh in view, resting on her full mouth, lingering unapologetically on the pale swell of her breasts above the towel.

'Drop the towel,' he said thickly.

Gloria was shocked into rigidity and quivered with incredulity. Nico regarded her expectantly. He was expecting that towel just to drop at his request. It was written all over him, in every poised line of his lounging stance.

Unintentionally, she crashed with burning black eyes and it was like having a blowtorch turned on her. Her mouth ran dry, her lungs struggled for oxygen. Heat flamed over her skin as it tightened over her bones, a tiny twisting sensation spiraling through her stomach. Her breasts felt peculiar, suddenly heavy, and full, her nipples stretching into almost painful sensitivity.

'You're so tiny and yet so perfectly proportioned,' he mused lazily in the pounding silence.

Gloria just couldn't believe that he was talking to her like this. Yet, on some subconscious level she wasn't surprised. This was Nico as she had never known him and yet as she had always known he could be. There was something dangerously fascinating about the raw sexual charge that came from him, the elemental throwback of a very physical male.

A 'predator', he had called himself with astonishing candor. And a predator he was, she registered.

'Would you please excuse me while I get dressed?' she murmured without any expression at all.

'You are not serious?' he breathed, as if she were the one behaving oddly.

Gloria shivered with fury, disgust flooding through her in waves. Nothing but bitterness, loathing and resentment lay between them, but Nico could obviously rise above all that to think about sex. Why? Purely because she was half-naked. Seemingly that was all it took to stoke the ever-glowing coals of Nico's powerful libido.

'I want to get dressed,' she said shakily.

'You're shy.' Nico tasted the word with purring satisfaction. 'And you have waited one hell of a long time for me.'

Gloria laughed. She couldn't help it. Laughter with a hysterical edge just spilled from her strained lips, shattering the silence like breaking glass.

'Stop it...'

Her clothes fell from her arms as she turned away and covered her contorted face with spread hands that were trembling. The hysteria had come from nowhere and attacked without warning.

She was furious that he should witness her loss of control. But she was even more devastated when she felt his arms close round her from behind. For a split-second she was so rigid that she imagined herself cracking under the stress of shock and breaking into pieces.

He was pulling her back into the hard, masculine heat of his body, threatening her with a disturbing physical contact she had never had. She couldn't believe that he was touching her. It was so unreal.

For five years this man had treated her like a leper. Now suddenly, when she was least equipped to deal with him, he was reaching out and touching as though that were his right. But it was not his right and she did not want his hands on her.

'Maybe you don't know where that certificate is,' Nico conceded half under his breath, lowering his dark head. 'Maybe he destroyed it, overlooked the copy. But maybe it's still out there in somebody's safekeeping, like a bomb waiting to be activated...'

His terminology made Gloria shiver. Nico was slowly, smoothly turning her round to face him. She had never fully appreciated how much stronger than a woman a man could be until Nico, impatient of her unresponsiveness, simply lifted her clear off the carpet and spun her like a doll back to him.

Barefoot she didn't even reach his shoulder and before he lowered her back down again her cheek brushed against his silk shirtfront as his jacket parted. Her breath caught in her throat, her nostrils flaring at the male scent of him, clean, citrusy...hot.

For a timeless moment her senses spun wildly, her lashes dipping as she was flooded by dizzy discomfiture.

'Look at me...' His accented voice could sound like sandpaper on silk.

'Please let me go,' she mumbled in a rush as she relocated her tongue.

She might as well not have spoken. Long fingers tilted up her chin and lingered there as she was involuntarily trapped by his blazing black eyes.

She knew as clearly as though he had spoken that the raging tension of the afternoon's events and his subsequent furious dissatisfaction had all been temporarily tossed on a back burner.

Far more basic urges were driving Nico now, a desire to vent all that pent-up tension in a fashion which she suddenly sensed would come as naturally to him as breathing.

Her skin prickled with a depth of awareness she would not have believed possible. The vibrations in the atmosphere were explosive.

'Nico...' Her own voice emerged clumsily, and she wanted to back off fast, but her feet were somehow connected to the carpet.

'It's so long since I heard you speak my name...' His intonation was deep pitched, disturbingly rough, lush ebony lashes low on a sliver of smoldering jet.

'No...' she heard herself whisper.

His thumb smoothed along the luscious curve of her lower lip, and she trembled, attempted to move, but his other hand was bent across her taut spine, holding her steady.

He watched her intently as he promised her lips apart with his thumb, intruded into the soft, damp interior, making her shiver violently as his palm cupped her delicate jawbone. It was the most insidiously erotic gesture she had ever experienced and set up a terrifying chain reaction through her treacherous body.

He was playing with her, tracking her every tiny response with a mixture of satisfaction and amusement. She understood that, read that in the eyes made famous by the financial press for being 'as unreadable as a blackout'.

He wasn't testing the water...no, indeed. Nico was neither humble nor uncertain. This was a male entirely acquainted with every seductive and sensual technique necessary to heighten his own pleasure and a male, similarly, given over to taking that pleasure whenever the mood took him.

'I want' her tongue felt too large for her mouth.

'More?' With devastating abruptness but immense cool, Nico released her and angled a sizzling smile down at her. 'Next time, drop the towel when I ask, ' he advised softly.

She would have found a blow less degrading than that insolent conclusion. As she heard the bedroom door snap quietly shut in his wake, Gloria went limp, her pallor pronounced. She had challenged him, angered him. She was shattered. All these years, nothing, and then...

Why now? She remembered him saying that her father could not force him into her bed as he had forced him into marriage. Her stomach twisted painfully. Mike was dead now. She had been available, in so much as she was female. Seemingly it took little else to attract Nico when he was in the mood for a little light sexual relief.

The peculiar way he had made her feel. Then that had been pure shock and nervous paralysis, Gloria told herself urgently. She had only been doing the sensible thing in not fighting, not arguing.

Nico was Italian and macho to the backbone. Telling him just at that moment either that she wanted a divorce or that she could not bear him to lay a single finger upon her might have been received like a thrown metal glove and it might well have encouraged him to attempt further intimacies. No, that had not been the right moment to mention Paul.

Gloria climbed back into her clothes, conscious that her hands were clumsy and still not quite steady. Then that was hardly surprising. Her husband had finally chosen to notice that she was alive.

Well, if not quite alive at least physically capable of providing the kind of entertainment he expected from her sex. She was disgusted, absolutely disgusted by his shameless disregard for decency in even daring to approach her!

Not only did he have no right to touch her, but he also wasn't even faithful to whomever he was with. He was made that way. A taker, not a giver. He had had a hard fight building his father's holdings up into the vast international power base that was the Julianne heritage today.

Nobody had done Nico any favors. So, he didn't do none. He went after his enemies like a warlord, slaughtered them and came back primitively victorious. He hid no light under a bushel, left no stone unturned in his fight for supremacy.

It was all those traits which her father had gloried in and dished up to her in suitable understatements to persuade her that though Nico had made no mention of love he would make her a wonderful husband.

Her mouth curved downwards in grim amusement. What husband? She had never had a husband. Five years ago, she hadn't had the benefit of a crystal ball.

Doubtless memory failed her for her recollection of their first meeting was radically different from his.

Before that day, Gloria had neither seen nor heard of Nico Julianne. She had just completed one term at finishing school, perfecting her technique with stupid flower arrangements. A course on men would have been far more useful, she reflected now.

Nico had appeared in the doorway of the conservatory, uninvited and unexpected. The maid had put him in the drawing-room to wait for her father and he must have seen her through the window because to get to the conservatory he had had to leave the drawing-room, cross the hall, go through another room, and enter the conservatory by the French windows there. So how come he'd accused her of setting him up for a meeting?

She had looked up and seen him in the doorway and, yes, at one glance had fallen head over heels in love with him. Nico had struck her as the most utterly gorgeous creation she had ever seen walk on two feet. He had stood there like a golden Italian god and her knees had wobbled, helpless excitement quivering through her.

'You are a breath of spring in this winter scene,' he had drawled almost stiltedly, dark eyes literally riveted to her. Yes, he had said it. Probably read it somewhere and memorized it for effect, but those most un-Nico-like words had indeed emerged from him.

Her pruning scissors had dropped from her nerveless fingers. He had picked them up and hovered. Yes, hovered, as though one part of him was urging him to retreat and another urging him to stay.

It had never occurred to Gloria that he had deliberately sought her out. She had assumed that he was interested in the plants and a conversation that years on should have filled her with laughter but somehow failed to do so had taken place. Nico had not revealed either his ignorance or his uninterest. He had asked appropriate questions and forced to conceal the fact that he had undoubtedly never touched or examined a plant in his life.

He had even told her that her eyes matched the genian violets, and that compliment had emerged almost as awkwardly as the first, giving

Gloria the impression that though he looked staggeringly sophisticated he was almost shy. Shy? Nico?

How much time had gone by in that conservatory? He hadn't mentioned his appointment with her father, indeed had given all the appearance of having forgotten it until the embarrassed maid had come in search of Gloria to tell her that her father wanted her and had been saddened to find Nico with her.

Gloria ate without even being aware of what she was eating. She felt guilty, exhausted, dismayingly confused. Her temples ached with strain. All her life she had been open and honest. Well, that was until three short months ago when Paul had accidentally sent her flying in Harrods.

Dishonesty was disgusting to her, but it hadn't occurred to her at the outset that she would become involved with him. He had insisted on taking her into the restaurant. They had laughed and chatted over coffee. Nothing could have been more innocent. The second meeting had been entirely accidental as well.

Pushing her plate away, Gloria gulped down a glass of wine, but it didn't take the nasty taste from her mouth. Why on earth did she feel like this? All she had to do was ask Nico for a divorce soon and it would all be over. Maybe she should stop seeing Paul until then. Was that what she should be doing? Or maybe she should just walk out and leave Nico a note to find the next time he was in New York. Cowardly, but probably all he deserved.

She was quite sure that Nico hadn't tormented over any of his women. He certainly hadn't cared about Gloria's feelings. Gloria had had to live with humiliation in the news as well as in private.

Nico was extremely photogenic and a gossip columnist's dream, the married man who led the adulterer's dream existence without any apparent interference from his wife. For Nico to say that he had been on a leash for five years was badly behaved nonsense. Then, two wrongs did not make a right. Why should she bend over to Nico's level?

Deciding against coffee, the exhaustion of extreme stress creeping over her like a suffocating blanket, Gloria decided to go to bed. Her strained mouth compressed when she remembered that she had no nightwear. The toweling robe hung in the bathroom for the use of guests was too bulky for comfort.

At the end she slid naked between the smooth sheets and in the comforting darkness she reached a decision. Tomorrow morning, she would tell Nico that she wanted a divorce. Then there would be no further need for her over-active conscience to torment her with this ridiculous sense of being in the wrong.

She awakened from a deep sleep with a start. The overhead lights were on full, and she blinked in complete disorientation as she sat up, momentarily not even recalling where she was. Then her sleepy eyes focused on Nico where he was poised several feet from the bed and flew wide. He looked like hell; that was her first thought as she clutched the sheet protectively round herself, belatedly recalling her nudity.

His dense black hair was tangled, his tie was missing and the white silk dress-shirt he wore beneath his dinner-jacket was half-open, displaying a disturbing wedge of bronzed chest, liberally sprinkled with curling dark whorls of hair. His strong, dark features were fiercely clenched and for someone of his usually vibrant skin tone he was staggeringly pale. Almost as though he was in shock, she thought uncertainly... severe shock.

"What's wrong...what time is it?" she mumbled, pushing a hand through the silken confusion of the silvery hair falling round her shoulders, swallowing back a yawn as she glanced at her watch to discover that it was the early hours of the morning.

'You have dishonored my name,' Nico breathed in what sounded more like broken English by virtue of the unusual thickness of his accent and his decidedly rough delivery.

Gloria cleared her throat and looked back at him, still not quite awake, fighting through the fog of her slow reactions. Eyes as black as pitch clashed on a violent collision course with hers and the explosive tension emanating from him in electrifying waves was finally communicated to her.

'Excuse me?' she muttered, certain that he couldn't possibly have said what she had thought he had said.

'My wife with another man...' He could hardly get the words out as he continued to stare at her with unwavering force as though she were some alien entities he had never seen before.

Ghostly fingers danced up her tight spinal cord. She tried and failed to swallow. But what ironically struck Gloria hardest was not his evident discovery that she had been seeing another man but that truly staggering designation of 'my wife', a label which until now Nico had never once been heard to voice.

In turn, Gloria found that same label almost unbelievably offensive, not to mention ridiculous in the context of their marriage.

'You do not deny it,' Nico murmured, every powerful angle of his lean body rigid with raw tension.

Gloria hugged the sheet, wondering dazedly why he was so angry. For shock she should have read disbelief. Had he expected her to sit there like some wet, faithful Angel forever, watching her life drain away into nothingness? All right, so she had been a doormat for a very long time, but surely even Nico could not have expected that to last indefinitely. In any case, what was it to him?

'How did you find out?' she asked, not as steadily as she would have liked, but fighting the intimidation of his dark, menacing attitude with all her strength.

'You do not even seem to appreciate the magnitude of your offence.' Nico studied her with outraged dark eyes and, if possible, he was even paler than he had been minutes earlier.

'Have you been drinking?' Gloria prompted weakly, wondering if that was what lay at the foot of such utterly unwarranted melodrama. Coming into her room in the middle of the night, confronting her like a wronged husband...how could he possibly consider himself wronged?

'What the hell has that to do with anything?' Moving an unwelcome step closer, Nico abruptly spread two lean hands in a violent arc of persuasive expression. 'I hear you on the phone with your lover. What I hear I cannot believe!'

'Oh.' Gloria bent her head. She should have guessed. But Nico was so naturally sneaky, he hadn't given a sign at the time.

She tried to recall what she had said but she couldn't, the conversation having been rushed and overshadowed by Nico's appearance. Well, she thought, sucking in a deep breath, it wouldn't have been the way she would have chosen for Nico to find out, but maybe it was for the best that it was all finally out in the open.

'I had the New York phone bills faxed to me and then I used the redial facility on the phone you had employed and checked it against the number you call most frequently.'

Sneaky didn't begin to describe him. An odd twisting sensation afflicted Gloria and she fought it, glancing up to say tightly, 'I would have told you about him if you had asked.'

'Tell me about him? Cristo...do you have no shame?'

Her chin came up. 'Why should I be ashamed?' But for some inexplicable reason his attitude was having that effect on her and that made her angry.

'You...are...my...wife,' Nico spelt out with a flash of even white teeth and an aura of pure violence, on the brink of being unleashed.

Instinctively, Gloria edged across to the far side of the bed, attacked by confusion and something that was coming dangerously close to fear despite her anger. When he said she was his wife she wanted to scream back at him that she was no more his wife than a stranger in the street, but his mood prevented her. He was scaring her. She didn't want to risk adding fuel to the fire.

'Perhaps you'll be feeling more reasonable in the morning.' She placed gentle stress on the last three words.

'Why?' Nico demanded in a low, simmering undertone, striding round the bed. 'Why would I be feeling more reasonable?'

As Gloria attempted to repeat the slippery maneuver, she had utilized mere seconds earlier, Nico disconcerted her entirely by suddenly coming down on the bed and clamping a bruising hand round her arm to hold her in place.

'What are you doing?' she shrieked in sudden panic.

He muttered something in Italian at her and pinned her down by her other arm as well when she attempted to pull free. White as a sheet, her teeth chattering with shock, she gazed up at him with frightened eyes.

Blazing black eyes bit down into her. 'How often have you been with him?'

'I...I didn't count.' Her mind was a total terrified blank.

Nico uttered with vicious intent. 'I will kill him... I will wipe him from the face of this earth! He's dead. He may still be walking around but he is dead.'

'Don't s-say things like that!' Gloria gasped in horror.

'And what about you? What do I do with you?'

'Me?' On the edge of hysteria and frozen there, Gloria stared up at him horrified. He was disturbed. That was the only possible explanation.

'Where did you meet him?'

'I'm not telling you anything about him!' she asserted, shivering as she recalled his threats.

'Paul Woods. He's twenty-eight. He's a would-be artist, part-time salesman. He's an only child, blond, blue-eyed, six feet tall and he is very ambitious. I don't need you to tell me any of that.'

Gloria was transfixed. The tip of her tongue snaked out to moisten her dry lips. She trembled. 'Why are you behaving like this? Why should it matter to you? I'm not your wife not really your wife...'

'Ohi...no?' he probed dangerously. 'You carry my name. You wear my ring. You live in my house. I feed you, I clothe you, I keep you.'

Mortified beyond bearing, Gloria reddened fiercely. 'And I hate you!'

'If that is true, you will hate me a lot more by the time I am finished,' Nico responded darkly in the pulsating silence.

'Let me go,' she whispered shakily.

'You will never see him again,' he swore, his eyes smoldering down at her in barely leashed rage.

In a sudden fluid movement, he shifted back from her, releasing her arms. 'But I will never forgive you for this...'

Feeling weak as a kitten, she slumped back against the pillows. Her reply just leapt off her tongue. 'That's OK,' she said. 'I'll never forgive you either.'

It was a mistake. Halfway to the door, Nico calmed and rolled back. 'So now you tell me the truth.'

'What truth?'

'That this is a deliberate attempt to attract my attention,' he condemned with shattering fury. 'No wonder you left track a blind man could follow...no wonder I am treated to an open door and the sound of you exchanging sweet nothings with your lover!'

'Attract your attention?' Gloria repeated, her elegant face alight with unhidden incredulity, physical weakness banished as she sat up in one abrupt movement.

'Which you have done beautifully,' Nico conceded with a sudden blazing smile that chilled her to the marrow.

'You haven't even slept with him, have you? So far and no further. Perfect.' He strolled back towards the bed, thrilling dark eyes questioning her with sarcastic brilliance. 'Not enough to send me over the edge but enough to make me sit back and take notice...'

Momentarily she was stunned by the utter depth of his conceit. Then she flung her head back, sapphire eyes flashing with fury. 'I have slept with him!' she lied hotly. 'And I don't want you over the edge or taking notice because I don't give a damn about you!'

'If he has laid one finger on your unclothed body, he's dead. You do understand that?' Nico examined her with hooded dark eyes, a deadly silence to his lean, powerful body. 'This is not some game. I warn you, if he's had you, I'll break him,' he declared with murderous cool.

Gloria couldn't move, couldn't breathe, couldn't credit that he could back her into a corner like that. How could he possibly guess that her relationship with Paul had yet to become intimate? She had lied in temper but also out of a need to stress that it was a serious relationship, not some silly flirtation manufactured to attract an indifferent husband's attention.

The very suggestion that she might be guilty of such childishly manipulative, not to say pathetic behavior made her blood boil in her veins. She was simultaneously terrified that Nico might harm Paul.

'You are having to think so hard about this, I feel almost embarrassed,' Nico revealed smoothly.

All the anger had gone as if it had never been, she registered in a daze. 'OK,' she muttered tightly, studying her tightly linked hands, hating Nico with so much venom that she was literally ill with the force of her feelings. 'I haven't slept with him.'

'And shall I tell you why? An Italian would divorce an unfaithful wife. So, you went as far as you dared and no further. The only reckless thing you ever did in your life was marry me. Cristo.'

Nico expelled his breathe in a hiss. 'What a fool I was to think for one second that you might risk losing your status as my wife!'

'But that's exactly what I want to lose!' Gloria shot back at him in unrestricted rage and frustration. 'I don't want you... I want my freedom!'

'Like hell you do,' Nico responded crushingly. 'You'd sink like a stone in the real world. You couldn't cut it out there. You'd be as helpless as a newborn baby without your credit cards!'

'How dare you?' Gloria spit out, white as snow.

A flying pitch-black brow elevated. 'I was just telling it like it is. You are exactly what Mike created: a beautiful, fragile ornament, the perfect wife for a very rich man, born to be waited on hand and foot...'

'You pig,' she gasped, pain tearing through her in a blazing wave.

'That's not to say that you're not very good in your own rarefied atmosphere,' he drawled in wry addition. 'You're a marvelous hostess. And you're a real lady. But if you really want your freedom'

'I do!' Gloria practically sobbed at him.

'Ask yourself why you're still buying my socks.' Unleashing a sardonic smile on her, Nico turned and strode out of the room.

What did his socks have to do with anything? That was just a trivial task she had taken on early in their marriage and kept on doing without even thinking about it!

Gloria dived out of bed, snatching up the toweling robe and digging her arms frantically into it. She had to make him listen. She had to make him understand.

He was in the master bedroom. Gloria halted on the threshold, discomfited to find him halfway out of his shirt.

'What now?' he grated with driven impatience.

'I want you to listen to me.' Twitching the neck of the robe higher with agitated fingertips, she made herself meet his unreadable gaze. 'I love Paul. I want a divorce.'

Nico strolled across the depth of the carpet towards her. 'You're my wife,' he delivered in a soft tone of revelation. 'And why are you, my wife? Because you so badly wanted to be my wife.'

A chaotic flush ran up her slender throat and her teeth clenched. 'Did you hear what I said? I love him!'

'You're buying his socks too?' Nico enquired without pause, savage amusement in his narrowed examination.

Without her even thinking about it, her hand flashed up and she slapped him hard, so hard that she couldn't feel her fingers for several tight seconds afterwards. Then she was shocked by what she had done, the unfamiliar violence which had simply surged up out of nowhere and spilt over.

Fearfully, she flinched back from him as he reached out for her, all amusement banished from his hard, dark eyes.

'No!'

'Even when I think a good slap might do you good, I can restrain myself. You're too small, too breakable. If I'd been the wife-beating type, don't you think you would have known it by now?'

Nico tugged her resistant body closer with easy strength, another kind of threat entirely explicit in the slow-burn effect of his dark gaze wandering over her, lingering on the steadily widening V of pale skin revealed by the far too large robe as it slid down off one narrow-boned shoulder.

'And I have to confess that my idea of entertainment is rather more intimate than violence and infinitely more satisfying.'

'Don't you dare touch me!' Gloria screamed so loudly that her voice cracked, and her throat hurt.

'A long, hot night in my bed is exactly what you need.' A lean hand settled on her bare shoulder.

'Don't be disgusting!' Gloria's facial muscles locked with revulsion.

'And don't dismiss out of hand what you have never experienced.' Nico laughed softly as he lowered his darkly handsome head and dragged her relentlessly up against him, one hand curving to the swell of her hips.

'Stop it.'

'I feel so threatened,' he mocked indolently, brushing a silvery strand of hair back from one delicate cheekbone in an almost tender gesture that struck her as so out of character that she found herself briefly losing track of her struggle for freedom.

'Nico...'

His mouth came down on hers with mesmerizing expertise and praised her soft lips apart. She stopped breathing. He gathered her closer, sealing her to every abrasively male angle of his taut body.

Her back arched without her volition, increasing that contact. His tongue drove into the moist, tender interior she had yielded and explored. A river of fire flowed through her, and she quivered, leaning against him, winding her arms sinuously round his neck.

Darkness waved behind her lowered eyelids, the heat in the pit of her stomach twisting like a hot wire through her trembling length.

Nico freed her swollen mouth and studied her with complete impassivity. 'What was his name?' he derided.

'His...oh, God!' On unsteady legs, Gloria went into retreat, her fingers flying up in stark distress and turmoil to her reddened lips.

'"Frailty, thy name is woman!"' Nico quoted with savage amusement. 'But you've got your priorities wrong. I'm the husband.'

Gloria struggled to think of something. Anything to say in self-defense. Nothing occurred to her. As she hovered, prey to several conflicting violent emotions, Nico shed his shirt, displaying powerful muscles that rippled like flexing cords beneath his golden skin. She didn't want to stare but she stared all the same.

Nico moved passed her, opened the door, and thrust her unceremoniously out into the corridor, murmuring, 'We'll talk over breakfast.'

The door pounded shut in her confused face. Was she going out of her mind? Had the past twenty-four tension-filled hours been a nightmare? She got back into bed, curled up in the fetal position and hugged herself.

Nico was a stranger. She didn't know him like this...and just for a little while she hadn't known herself either. He had been so bitter, so angry at the bank. He had devastated her. But since then, his every switch of mood had caught her by surprise. It was as if there were a script running somewhere and she was the only one who hadn't read it yet.

He had bubbled with rage when he'd realized that she had been seeing another man. He had scared her half out of her wits. But as long as the affair had been arrested outside the bedroom door, he was able to shrug it off with the truly astonishing belief that she had only been trying to make him sit up and take notice of her.

Suddenly, he was being sarcastic rather than furious, assuring her that she couldn't survive except as his wife and revealing with every following word and action the most staggering revelation of all...

Nico didn't seem to want a divorce. Gloria found that totally and unbelievable in the circumstances. Why would he want to hang on to a wife he had been blackmailed into marrying? Why would he want to hang on to an empty charade?

It didn't make sense; it didn't make any sense at all. Her every expectation had been torn from her and she felt like somebody trying to walk a tightrope in the dark. Nico was unpredictable. OK, but this was something else again and she couldn't sleep for wondering what was motivating him and why all of a sudden, he was making sexual advances to a wife he had casually ignored for five years.

Even worse was trying to figure out why she hadn't fought him off, why she had just stood there and allowed him to kiss her and felt so hot and that she could have died with shame afterwards.

Nico was very experienced. Maybe any male, possessed of that brand of carnal expertise, could tempt a woman as inexperienced as she was. Maybe it was all a matter of pressing the right physical buttons. Even so, he had still dragged a response from her far more powerful than Paul had ever managed.

Don't, she screamed inside her head, guilty and thoroughly ashamed of herself. How could there be any comparison? Sex was the least important thing in a relationship, to her way of thinking. She loved Paul; she did love Paul. Nico had shaken that belief not at all.

She was badly shaken by the unwelcome discovery that she could still be exposed after all this time to Nico's undeniable sexual charisma. She had thought she had grown out of that. She had thought she was safe, cured, indifferent. He had taught her otherwise and laughed. Dear God, laughed. She relived the moment, racked by the torment of her shattered pride.

A case was sitting just inside the door when she woke up, feeling like a corpse. Nico had had fresh clothing flown in. Oh, so thoughtful of him. Gloria dress in the dark blue Versace suit, spent longer than usual striving to repair the ravages of a virtually sleepless night and only emerged from the bedroom when she felt she had achieved the miracle.

Nico was relaxing back in his chair behind the Financial Times. He lowered it, cast it aside and lifted his coffee. 'You should go back to bed. You look like a vampire victim waiting on the third bite.'

'Very funny,' Gloria gritted, a flush driving away the pallor which had made the blusher on her cheeks stand out.

An ebony brow quirked. 'I think you're incredibly lucky still to be all in one unbruised, attached piece after what I found out last night. I think I have been remarkably tolerant and understanding, but don't push it.'

Gloria snatched at a croissant, conscious of night-dark eyes tracking her every movement. He was engraved in her mind's eye. Immaculate in a navy pinstriped suit and red silk tie. No bags under his eyes. No visible sign of last night's horrors tarnished his natural enthusiasm. Her nerves were shattered, and he was as laid-back and in control as he had ever been.

In fact, he looked very arrogant. Hatred coursed through her. Her hands shook as she tore apart the croissant.

'I intend to see a solicitor this morning,' she announced without looking at him. 'I want a divorce.'

'In your dreams,' Nico said softly.

Her silver head shot up. 'I…'

'Shut up,' Nico told her with hard emphasis.

'You can't prevent me.'

'I'll just pretend I didn't hear that.'

'And I'm not going to sit here and be insulted.'

'Sit down!' he bit out, his hard voice cracking like a whiplash down the table at her. Gloria got such a shock that she sat again. 'I want you to listen to me.'

She sugared her coffee, refusing to look up. Let him have his say. He was not going to stop her starting a divorce. She was entitled to her freedom and nothing he could do or say was likely to stop her reaching out and simply grabbing it.

'Five years ago, I was twenty-five and you were seventeen, a very young seventeen. A child inside a woman's body. I don't get all hot and excited at the idea of sleeping with an adolescent, even if she is my wife! I found that a complete turn-off,' Nico delivered with painful candor. 'Some men like very young girls. I'm not one of them.'

Gloria kept on stirring her coffee. She was very pale, painfully embarrassed, and oddly guilty that it had never once crossed her mind that Nico might feel that way about the teenaged bride, he had had forced on him. 'You hated me anyway,' she said tightly.

'I resented you. I don't think I ever got as far as hating you. I just closed you out,' Nico mused. 'We were stuck with each other, and I dealt with it my way.'

'Excuse me if I throw up,' Gloria inserted jerkily, unable to still the juvenile response but suddenly obviously conscious of just how juvenile she had sounded. Nor did she want the past raked up, she registered uneasily.

There was so much pain and turmoil there. She might have learned to put it behind her, but he was dragging up very raw memories...

'I started work when I was fourteen on one of my father's ships. He was an old-fashioned man. He wanted me to start at the bottom and work up because he had done it that way.

I knew I needed an education. The next eight years were filled with eighteen-hour days. When I wasn't slogging my guts out, I was studying to try and keep up and playing the stock market on the side. I didn't have a misspent youth. I didn't have time for one,' Nico completed drily.

He had never talked to her like this before. It disturbed her. She lifted her coffee-cup and hugged it to her, finding some kind of security in its warmth. She had had a rough idea of what his early years had been like, but she hadn't realized they had been quite as grim and joyless as he made them sound. 'I don't know why you're telling me this.'

'I want you to understand what it was like for me being forced into marriage when I wasn't ready for it.'

'I understand perfectly,' Gloria said frigidly.

'I had finally reached the top. I was at last free to do everything I never got to do when I was younger,' he asserted in a driven undertone.

'You were free to sleep around,' Gloria rephrased with icy distaste. 'And then Mike came along and saddled you with me, right?'

'Yes, if you must put it like that, but I did not sleep around. You're a woman. You couldn't possibly understand what it is like for a man. It is a stage every man must go through, but I went through it later than most.'

Sexist toad, she thought bitterly, drinking down her coffee in one gulp. There was a whole world of gasping, gushing women out there and she sincerely doubted that he had left one willing woman unexplored.

Apart from his wife, Gloria had been left in frozen animation, denied everything he took by right for himself. Stowed away on a shelf to shrivel up in an empty, echoing New York house where even the servants were foreign. A consuming bitterness assailed her.

'I get the picture. As insidious an excuse for adultery as any woman has ever received. In fact, it's so damned brilliant, you really ought to go public with it!'

'I am not apologizing for myself. I married you under threat. I would not have married you otherwise. I was not ready to make that commitment to any woman at twenty-five.' Smoldering black eyes smashed into hers with unashamed force. 'It was better that I left you alone than shared your bed and strayed as I probably would have done.'

'I don't doubt it.' Gloria seems trembling with a combustible mix of emotions: rage, resentment, hatred and remembered pain and humiliation. She physically hurt with the control it took to hold them in.

Nico watched her from below lush ebony lashes. 'And then there was the obscene idea of performing like a stud for Mike's benefit.'

Gloria reddened as though he had slapped her across the face.

'On many occasions I have looked at you over the last couple of years and been very tempted to take you to my bed, but it would have been like surrendering to the enemy and I doubt if you would have enjoyed the effect that had on me.'

'I really don't want to hear any more,' she admitted tightly.

Nico ignored her. 'But now Mike is gone. I may not have that certificate as yet but I don't believe you know where it is...or even what it is.'

'You wouldn't believe how relieved I feel. Tell me, is there some point to this deeply unpleasant walk down memory lane?' Gloria prompted stiffly.

Nico treated her to a ravenous smile. 'I'm ready to settle down into being married.'

Her breath escaped in an audible hiss. Her lashes flickered. Incredulous sapphire-blue eyes clung to his darkly handsome features, her heartbeat sitting about her shaken throat.

Chapter 16

Returning to New York

'You look as if you need a good, stiff drink.' Rising gracefully upright, Nico strode across to the polished antique sideboard, extracted a brandy goblet and calmly poured a measure from the cut-glass decanter. With incredible cool, he settled it down on the table in front of her and strolled across to the marble fireplace.

You can't be serious,' Gloria told him, dry-mouthed.

'Apart from the smear of your family tree, you're everything I want in a wife.'

'Forgive me if I find that impossible to believe.'

'You're beautiful, sexually appealing and you're already mine,' he drawled with wry amusement. ' I haven't met anyone else one half as suitable.'

'Thanks, but no, thanks.' Shaken to her innermost depths by the proposition, Gloria was bereft of the wit to come back with anything more sarcastic.

'I don't recall saying you had the right of refusal. I'm prepared to be reasonable. I proved that last night.' Nico dealt her a razor-sharp glance of explicit meaning. 'I could have flattened you down on my bed there and then…'

'No!' Gloria rose upright, rigid with rejection.

'But I didn't. I'll give you time to adjust to the idea. I don't expect you to behave as though the last five years never happened.'

'I love Paul.'

' I don't expect to hear his name on your lips again. I warned you. That is over. You're allowed one mistake; one bitter little fling and you've had it.' Nico ran hooded dark eyes grimly over her pale, set face. 'One mistake,' he repeated in case she hadn't got the message.

'Phone him, go near him again and I'll break both of you because whether you like it or not, you're my wife!'

'You can't do that...you can't threaten me!'

'That wasn't a threat, that was a cast-iron promise. Cross the boundary lines I set and take the consequences. Don't say you weren't warned,' he murmured with chilling emphasis. 'Don't think that because I was tolerant last night, I'll be tolerant again. I won't be.'

'You can't make me stay with you.'

'Try me; step out of line and see what happens,' he invited darkly, scanning her with angry black eyes. ' Don't kid yourself that you've found true love. Woods has a history of chasing wealthy women.'

'He didn't even know I was wealthy!' Gloria spat at him furiously.

'He'd have to be blind not to. Look at your jewelry...look at your clothes! Why do you think you have a bodyguard? You're a walking invitation for every mugger for miles around!

That bracelet on your wrist is worth more than he could earn in a lifetime!' he slashed back. 'And he needn't think you'd be bringing your father's blood money with you because you will be signing your entire inheritance away to charity.'

'Really?' she gasped.

'You want to keep it? Profit from all the misery he caused his victims?'

Sick to the stomach at the idea, Gloria slung him a frustrated look of loathing and turned away.

'You will return New York to pack. We're flying to Italy in forty-eight hours.'

'Italy?' she echoed.

'It's time you meet my family.'

'No way am I staying married to you and no way am I going to Italy!'

'Go take a long, cool shower and concentrate on the absence of options available,' Nico advised drily.

'When you've finished doing that, think about how long Woods lingered in your dizzy brain when you were in my arms last night.'

'You bastard...' It was a derogatory term she had never used before, a word she had never liked, but it came out all the same.

Nico calmed down. 'And why do you call me that?'

She went icy cold under the onslaught of his savage gaze.

'Why?' he persisted.

'Well, why not?' Gloria backed away, shocked by the menacing vibrations stirring up the atmosphere around them. 'You swine...' she fumbled stupidly.

'I can live with that one.' His intense gaze veiled, his expressive mouth compressing. 'Gloria, we could have a very good marriage. Keep that in mind.'

'You have to be joking,' she muttered tightly.

'I realize that the martyr mentality has got a good grip on you, but I'm asking you to give us a chance.'

Her bewildered eyes flickered over his tight features. She marked the fierce determination etched there, recognized the suppressed emotion framing his dark drawl.

His tension sprang out at her, as though he felt he was putting his pride on the line in making such a request. It shook her, unsettled her on some level she was reluctant to probe. Hurriedly she turned away in silence.

'Gloria, do you want the information I have on Woods?'

Her stomach heaved. Dear God but Nico, was unscrupulous. How on earth had he planned to find out so much about Paul late last night? But then, money talks, didn't it?

The few facts might have been correct, but the rest was lies. Lies it suited Nico to tell, and cheap at the price if they undermined her faith in the man she loved. Nico did not know how strong that love was. How could he? Love didn't enter his requirements for marriage or his extra-marital activities.

How could he even begin to understand what it had been like for her to emerge from the emotional desert of her loneliness, her sense of inadequacy? Paul was interested in her. He listened to her, encouraged her, supported her. He cared about her in a way a man like Nico could never care.

She would not let that go, she swore to herself, not her one chance in life to love and be loved. Nico could find a dozen women to satisfy his wifely requirements. Looks, physical appeal, the ability to be a good hostess and no doubt a commensurate ability to turn a blind eye when her husband strayed into other beds just one of those male things, you know, something no mere woman could possibly understand!

Well, the tolerant wife wouldn't be Gloria! She had no doubt at all that he would be flooded by a rush of eager applicants, ninety per cent of whom would be far more prepared for the downside of being married to Nico than Gloria had been at seventeen!

A migraine headache attacked when she was on the flight back to New York. She stumbled sickly through the airport, fell into the waiting limousine, and practically crawled into the house.

Upstairs in her beautiful bedroom suite, her maid took one look at her pain-racked, perspiring face and rushed to close the curtains and help her down on to the bed. When she was alone, she cried, tears seeping down silently from her lowered eyelids, dripping on to the pillow. She was beyond thought, beyond anything but simple reaction.

Next morning, her strength returned and, along with it, her determination. She made plans and acted on them. The only piece of jewelry she possessed which was truly hers had belonged to her maternal grandmother. It was a cobweb-fine diamond necklace, and she was extremely attached to it. But it was her only passport to freedom.

She had to have cash to live on until she found her feet. It might be news to Nico, she reflected bitterly, but she understood it would be very tough for her to find those feet.

When she walked out of Nico's house, she wasn't taking any of the trappings of the old life with her. No credit cards, no fancy clothes, no jewelry.

She intended to make it on her own. She had no right to his money or his financial support. After all, she had never been his wife. Why should she go for a divorce when she could seek an annulment? Her marriage had been born out of blackmail, out of dark secrets and threats. Its dissolution would be as plain and honest as Leah could make it.

She sold her grandmother's necklace in a jeweler. It hurt; it filled her with guilt, but she hoped that if the mother she barely remembered was looking down she would understand her daughter's desperation.

Back at the house, she started to clear out her wardrobes in search of plainer, more casual clothes jeans, T-shirts, sweaters, skirts. She would go to a small hotel until she could find cheaper accommodation.

Then, she was going to get a job, any job. It didn't matter how boring. As helpless as a newborn baby? No way!

The internal phone rang. It was Peter, informing her that she had a visitor downstairs. A Mr. Woods. Paul had come to the house. Gloria was shaken. When he hadn't phoned last night, she had assumed he was out, and had intended to ring him later when she had finally accomplished her removal from Nico's house.

Paul was standing in the drawing-room, studying a Picasso drawing, Nico's one artistic weakness.

'You shouldn't have come here!'

'Is it real?' He indicated the drawing.

'Yes.' She had so much to tell him, she didn't know where to start, didn't know what she should tell, what she should keep to herself. There was, she discovered in confusion, an odd vein of loyalty to Nico somewhere inside her.

She didn't like to see Paul in Nico's house. It just didn't seem right. Maybe that was why she didn't feel she could throw herself into Paul's arms.

'I was told you weren't home when I tried to phone you last night,' He revealed, tight mouthed.

'But I was.' Was Nico responsible for that development? Were even her calls to be screened and censored now? But then she reminded herself that it didn't matter anymore. She was leaving. 'I've told Nico I want a divorce,' she imparted tautly.

'I'm moving out today.'

Paul's handsome face split into a wide grin. He crossed the carpet in one stride and grabbed her. 'Darling, that's fantastic!'

As he attempted to kiss her, Gloria angled her head back out of reach, her nervous tension rocketing. 'Not here...it doesn't feel right,' she muttered shakily.

Paul laughed. 'I hope it feels better in my apartment tonight.' He kept his arms linked round her.

'Paul...' Gloria swallowed hard. 'I'm not moving in with you.'

He frowned and then his brow cleared. 'It might count against you in the divorce...you're right. Sensible girl.

After the hell he's put you through, why should you pose as the guilty partner? It might affect your settlement.'

'I don't want Nico's money.'

Paul's bright blue eyes narrowed. 'Don't be silly, Gloria. I know you already have your father's inheritance but...'

Gloria tensed. Why was all the talk about money? 'A history of chasing wealthy women'... Nico's jibe returned to her. Angrily she thrust it away. 'We'll have to talk about that.'

'I'm only thinking about you. You're not used to roughing it. I couldn't bear to feel I was dragging you down.'

'You wouldn't be. I'll be free and we'll be just like any other couple,' she reasoned in a rush. 'You should go now. You shouldn't be here...'

'Relax, for God's sake.' Paul was wandering round the room, taking careful account of the antique furniture, and scrutinizing the remainder of the pictures. 'How much of this stuff is yours?' he enquired, with a low whistle of admiration.

Gloria heard the tone of suppressed excitement, saw the greedy look on his face and something died inside her. All Paul seemed able to think about was what she would bring with her.

Her deadened eyes fell on her mother's elegant little writing desk, passed on to her by her father after her wedding, the only piece of furniture in the entire house which belonged to her.

Something buzzed at the back of her mind as she looked at it but she was too upset by what she had just seen in Paul to be able to concentrate.

'None of its mine. In fact, I signed a pre-nuptial agreement before my marriage and I don't get anything,' she lied shakily. 'And the problem in Paris with my father's estate? I'm afraid that money must go towards settling his debts...'

'Debts?' Paul gaped at her. 'You're having me on.'

'No; when I walk out of this house, I'll be penniless.'

'But you never told me that!' he condemned, and then fell suddenly silent. His mouth compressed. 'You shouldn't move out without giving it very careful thought. God knows, I'm only thinking of what's best for you.'

'Of course,' she managed.

'I would feel really bad if you gave all this up purely for my benefit.' His smooth insincerity twisted her stomach. 'I mean, suppose it didn't work out between us? I must be honest. I'm not sure I could handle that responsibility. We both need to think very carefully about what we're doing.'

He said he had an appointment. He wanted to extract himself without embarrassment and consider over what she had told him. It felt like a robot, was scared to feel again. You fool, you fool, echoed at the back of her head. She had fallen for the first smoothie to pay her attention.

Of course, Paul had listened, supported, encouraged. He had flattered her battered pride, buttered her up with compliments. Naturally. He had wanted her to leave Nico but only if she brought Nico's money with her.

She went back upstairs and worked frantically to complete her packing. Nothing had changed, she told herself. Paul might no longer figure in her future, but she didn't want Nico there either.

She was finished with Nico, finished with the past. She damned well didn't need any man to lean on! Three in a row. Her father, Nico, and Paul. All of them using, manipulating, abusing. What had she done? She had put up as much resistance as a boneless, brainless rag doll! Her anger was so great, she could hardly contain it.

Her cases downstairs, she called a cab.

'I won't be needing anyone,' she said, and when they argued, she added, 'I'm leaving him.'

Everybody would know soon enough, she reasoned…

The cab came. As it drove off, she took a last look back at the house and it was scary knowing that she was leaving security behind. The cab driver was very helpful about suggesting a hotel. She checked in and went out immediately to buy a newspaper. Finding somewhere to stay and a job were her only priorities.

A knock on the door of her room sounded at ten that night. Gloria slid off the bed and unlocked the door. She took one devastated look at Nico and attempted to shut it again. His golden features taut and furious, he planted a hand against the door and thrust it back to the wall, forcing her to retreat.

'How the hell did you know where I was?'

'Boyce had the wit to follow you.' Nico leaned back against the door and locked it.

'He had no right to do that,' she said bitterly.

'He works for me and you're a prime target for kidnapping. He did what he had to do,' Nico bit out. 'Just as I'm about to do what I have to do.'

Gloria stiffened, clashing with murderous black eyes. 'And what's that supposed to mean?'

'I'm not letting you go,' he breathed fiercely.

Pain slivered through her but her sapphire eyes gleamed with contempt. 'You're like a dog with a bone you buried and forgot about. You had no interest in that bone until somebody else dug it up!'

'You are my wife.'

'Since when? Since when was I your wife? You think feeding and clothing covers it?' Gloria jibed helplessly. 'Well, you can keep your clothing and your food and your rotten money because I don't want any of it. Any more than I want you!'

'You always wanted me...'

'You missed the boat. I got over you a long time ago,' Gloria flung with a sort of disillusioned enjoyment that was new to her.

'But you still want me to pay,' Nico slotted in, strolling fluidly closer. Shimmering dark eyes assailed hers with force, the anger he was controlling blatant in that hard stare.

'So, you walk out without even telling me. I didn't even qualify for a note.'

'And what did you expect? Dear Nico, it's been a lousy five years, goodbye? That's about all I could have to say to you!'

'You brought him into my house,' Nico murmured roughly.

Gloria calmed down, her hectic color sliding away, utterly silenced by the news that he was aware of Paul's visit.

'And no doubt if it had suited you would have taken him to our bed as well!'

An edged laugh was torn from Gloria. The smoldering tension in the atmosphere was so thick she could taste it but she refused to be intimidated. This confrontation was long overdue.

Finally, she was having her say. 'We never had a bed, so fulfilling that ambition would have been a little difficult!'

'Stop it,' Nico grated, a tiny muscle pulling at the corner of his compressed mouth. 'I am trying not to lose my temper.'

'I don't want you and your temper in this room. I want you to leave…'

'Not without you.'

'Why? What's so special about me?' Leah demanded tempestuously, out of control as she had never been before, her stormy emotions feasting on every acid word.

'Why don't you marry one of your bimbos, Nico? Or am I missing something here? Were the bimbos as much of a front as our marriage was? You see, I am not as dumb as I used to be. Why do you want me to stay so badly? Could it be that you're gay?'

The instant she said it she regretted it. She hadn't meant to go that far in her need to lash out. A shudder ran through Nico, naked outrage flashing across his savagely handsome features.

'No…not gay,' he bit out with considerable effort. As he spoke, he shrugged off his jacket and ripped at his tie. 'Maybe you need a demonstration…'

Gloria blinked, her blinding surge of rage having vented itself on that final accusation which she was guiltily aware had, for Nico, been the ultimate insult. 'What are you doing?'

'Something I should have done years ago.' He tore his shirt out of his beautifully tailored trousers and pulled it over his dark head, discarding it in a heap with the rest.

'Would you please put your clothes back on?' Gloria said unsteadily, and she knew she sounded ridiculous, which didn't help.

'Scared you'd see something you might like? Cristo…' Nico intoned rawly. 'To think I was about to waste time courting my wife! To think I was going to do stupid things like buying you flowers and taking you out! Get on that bed…'

'Have you gone crazy?' Gloria gasped in disbelief.

Before she could move, Nico caught her up in his powerful arms and dumped her down on the sofa behind her. He came down on top of her so fast that she hadn't a hope of evading him. Waves of shock coursed through her.

'You're my wife,' Nico growled down at her, as if that were sufficient justification.

'Let go of me...you're flattening me!' Gloria slung back at him in fury.

'Maybe you'll get to like it.' Nico shifted sinuously above her and meshed one hand into her tumbled hair. He stared down at her for a long, timeless moment. 'God, I am so hungry for you, I ache,' he muttered raggedly.

Gloria's entire body was an angry pillow of rejection. 'Go find a bimbo, Nico,' she urged shakily. 'At least you won't have to tell her lies.'

'I'm not lying. How could I? A man's body betrays his arousal.' Sliding a lean thigh between hers, Nico moved against her, shamelessly introducing her to the hard bulge of his manhood. 'No lie,' he completed huskily.

Pink starred her cheeks even as an insidious heat flared between her thighs. 'You're disgusting.'

'I want you.' He buried his mouth hotly in a hollow just below her collarbone.

'No!' she whispered frantically, feeling that hot wire of sensation pull tight and reacting in panic.

He lifted his dark head, a blaze of desire in his hot gaze, and then he took her mouth with explosive passion. It was an act of possession, a stamp of ownership blatant in its intent to dominate. She knew it, fought what he was making her feel with every fiber, but with every kiss, with every sweetly invasive thrust of his tongue, he taught her to want the next. Her hands rose, curved compulsively to the satin-smooth skin of his shoulders, holding him to her.

He rolled over, carrying her with him, and dispensed with her T-shirt by whipping it over her head. He uttered a savage groan as her unbound breasts rubbed against his hair-roughened chest and a split-second later she was lying flat again, his hands shaping the pouting mounds he had discovered.

She shut her eyes, gasping for breath, all reasoning power wrested from her. He found a swollen pink nipple with his mouth, and she dug her hips into the mattress, her back arching, a wildness she had never known tearing at her. Her heart was racing, her skin damp, every cell firing on red alert.

He employed his tongue and his teeth in a grazing torment of a caress, cupping her breasts, sucking at the sensitive buds he had aroused. She speared her fingers into the depths of his thick, silky hair and moaned with the intensity of the pleasure.

'You are mine,' Nico grated in a voice so tortured that she didn't initially realize that he had spoken in English.

She wasn't listening anyway. He was apart from her. She didn't like it. She lifted her head and touched his sensual mouth with her lips and then, more daringly, with the tip of her tongue, unconsciously imitating what she had learned from him.

He shuddered and accepted the invitation with a raw passion that consumed her, his arms banding so tightly around her that she could barely breathe.

They rolled over again, joined together by an increasingly uncontrollable excitement. She heard something rip. It meant nothing to her. She was lost entirely in the heat and the scent and the feel of him.

He felt so hot. His scent was sexy that sent her senses spinning. Every tiny shift of his lean, muscular body against hers drove her wild, every caress an incitement to a hunger fast reaching fever pitch.

Her breasts had become incredibly sensitive, and he played with the tender flesh with every atom of erotic expertise in his repertoire. His fingers flirted with the damp tangle of curls at the base of her tight stomach, and she panted for oxygen and then moaned helplessly as his heated exploration roved to the very heart of her.

She couldn't be still, couldn't control her own extremities. The wild pulsebeat of desire had taken her over. Her hips jerked up in a rhythm she didn't know but somehow found, her head thrown back, her slender throat extended. An intolerable ache was building up, making her sob out his name repeatedly.

Nico said something in Italian and groaned against her reddened mouth like a man in torment. 'I can't wait.'

Then he was there where she most wanted him to be, pushing up her thighs with wildly impatient hands, sliding against the honeyed welcome he had prepared for himself. Her eyes flew wide, passion-glazed sapphire locking with burning jet.

She tensed. She could feel him, hot and smooth and hard, suddenly threateningly male. She searched his rigid features and saw such a look of vulnerability momentarily etched in those beautiful eyes that her heart lurched. Suddenly, she wanted him so badly it hurt.

He entered her with a stifled groan, slowly, gently, and the pain she was braced to withstand was merely a fleeting stab of discomfort, quickly past and forgotten under the storm of fiery sensation which engulfed her. Instant meltdown.

Every thrust lifted her higher, burning out everything but the feeling, submerging her in the hungry demand of her own need. He moved faster and she wrapped her arms round him, out of control, her heart pounding, her pulses racing, and then it happened, an explosion of white-hot heat flying up inside her, sending her out of her mind with its strength.

Nico drove into her violently and then shuddered with the force of his own release.

Blissfully pliant, still floating gloriously slowly back to earth, Gloria snuggled into him as he slid onto his side, every quivering curve glued to him.

She pressed her lips to a muscular brown shoulder, nostrils flaring at the musky damp scent of him. The light went out. Silence fell. Gloria wandered over the edge of complete exhaustion into sleep, sprawled on top of him.

Chapter 17

Elena and Nico

Nico's voice, talking in Italian, but she was in bed. Her feathery lashes shot up, revealing startled sapphire-blue eyes. Her arrested attention fell on Nico. He had his back turned to her. He was standing at the window, one lean hand occupied by a mobile phone. Shock rolled over her in a debilitating wave. A Technicolor replay of the events of the night before sizzled through her brain, not a single X-rated second deleted.

She couldn't explain how it had happened. That was the most appalling discovery of all. One minute she had been screaming at him in fury, the next...? As she stiffened below the crumpled sheet, unfamiliar muscles complained, and a faint ache intimately reminded her of the explosive passion which had flared up between them.

Hot color burnished her cheeks. Had Nico not still been physically present, she would have believed it was all a dream... A nightmare, she amended with a shudder. She rubbed at her temples, vaguely conscious that her head was sore, her throat slightly raw.

Join the bimbo fraternity, she told herself with sudden fury. But join at the bottom of the class...

The average bimbo had a certain native cunning, knew where she was going and how. Gloria had fallen at the first major obstacle. She had finally got up the courage to leave Nico, had felt good about that decision, indeed had felt empowered by it...and then he had brought her down on this bed and kissed her and inexplicably the balance of power had swung violently back to the enemy; for he was the enemy.

Anyone capable of reducing her to this level was the enemy. As she moved her head on the pillow, it swam.

Her tortured gaze rested on him, on the angle of his well-shaped dark head, the breadth of his shoulders beneath the fine cloth of his jacket, the jut of his narrow hips as he dug a lean hand into the pocket of his tailored trousers and bent his long legs.

She was shattered by just how much she liked looking at him, how familiar every gesture was, every fluid change of stance. Pain traversed her tight features. She knew then how it had happened.

She had blocked out Nico's attraction, blocked out the hunger, blocked out every thought of him. Self-preservation had taught her to do that. But all along that attraction had still been there, a sexual craving denied and buried and made more dangerous by that suppression.

It was that same craving which had escaped and betrayed her in Nico's arms. Given the opportunity, she had grabbed him...just as he had always said she would.

Hot moisture lashed the back of her eyelids, but she wouldn't let the tears fall. She really didn't feel well but that was no good reason to give way to such weakness.

Nico turned and strolled across to the bed. He was too much of a predator not to smile, his sensual mouth curving with self-satisfaction as he looked down at her. He couldn't even hide it. He settled down on the edge of the mattress, lustrous dark eyes tracking over her intently. 'It's a beautiful morning.' She could hear the wind lashing the rain against the windows.

'In Italy,' he added softly, lifting a hand, and skating a finger along the taut line of her lower lip. 'And if you tell me you're not coming. No, don't you dare tell me that,' he warned as her lips began to part. 'Not after last night.'

'That was just sex,' Gloria bit out, a spicy flush staining her skin. His smile merely grew in brilliance as he lowered his dark head. 'Never just sex,' he reproved huskily. 'Fabulous, wonderful, incredible sex. If the jet wasn't on stand-by, I'd still be in bed.'

Her teeth gritted. 'Yesterday, I left you.'

'Today we are closer than we have ever been. Life is so unpredictable,' Nico pointed out with immovable self-assurance. 'Think of this as the first day of our marriage.'

'That is the most nauseating suggestion I've ever heard!' Gloria snapped, hounded beyond bearing. 'I don't want to go to Italy.'

Nico slid upright. 'But you will. My family are all gathering to meet you at my mother's home. I don't care if I must drag you kicking and screaming all the way to the airport,' he delivered with sudden harshness, his strong jawline clenching. 'To be blunt, you made your decision last night!'

'You did it deliberately!' Gloria gasped.

'Yes.' The unvarnished affirmative was like a slap in the face. 'Now why don't you get dressed? I instructed your maid to pack for you. I assume that what you have here wasn't planned with Italy in mind.'

Wrapping herself awkwardly in the sheet under Nico's grimly amused gaze, Gloria was conscious of her swimming head and for the first time acknowledged that she really wasn't feeling well at all.

She went into the bathroom. This was her penance, that was what it was. Her punishment for stupidity. The knowledge that she had helplessly connived in her own downfall was a bitter pill to swallow.

Gloria made herself swallow it, trailing out every thought, every feeling with masochistic candor.

She had believed she was in love with Paul. Had Paul been her escape route from her marriage? Deep down had she needed the belief that someone loved her to work up the courage to leave Nico.

The idea that she was loved had given her strength, had restored her faith in herself. But yesterday she had been forced to face reality.

Paul hadn't loved her...but had she loved him? For a while he had made her feel good about herself. Yesterday, she had seen through his superficial charm so clearly that she had marveled that she had ever been taken in.

Yes, it had been very painful, having to accept that he had viewed her as a purely profitable enterprise. But did she still long for him? No, there had been a terrible finality to the sense of alienation she had felt. She never wanted to see Paul again. So, had she ever loved him? Or had it been an infatuation born of her loneliness?

Lord, the bathroom was hot. Gloria sank down dizzily on the side of the bath during trying to dress herself. She felt as weak as a kitten and light-headed. It was becoming an immense challenge to concentrate but still she forced herself to the task.

Last night had been a ghastly mistake. Did she now hang her head in shame and let Nico browbeat her into staying with him even though she felt that that was the very worst thing she could do?

She lifted an unsteady hand to her pounding temples and knew she had to make herself strong, knew she had to stand up for herself.

Emerging from the bathroom, she leaned back against the doorframe for support. Nico surveyed her with narrowed eyes. 'What's wrong?'

'I think I've got the flu...but that's not important.' Breathing in to sustain herself, she stared sickly back at him. 'I'm staying here...not coming back to you.'

'You're not feeling well. You don't know what you're saying,' Nico cut in. 'I'll take you down to the car.'

'No!' she gasped, tears of frustration and weakness gathering in her eyes as her wobbling lower limbs threatened to collapse under her. 'Don't you ever listen? You're wrong for me!'

Nico swept her up in his arms despite her feeble attempt to evade him.

'Please!' Her failure to get through to him or persuade him to put her down again drove her crazy. 'I don't want to go with you. I want to stay here.'

'God… you're expecting him, aren't you?' he raked down at her with barely restrained anger. 'If you weren't sick, I'd shake you!'

Her cases were already gone, she saw in horror as Nico thrust open the door of her room, holding her steady with one powerful arm.

'Let me go!' Her swimming head fell back against his shoulder as he strode down the corridor.

'If I let you go, you'll fall in a heap at my feet.' He muttered something deep in Italian, his set, dark features as unyielding as stone as he hit the call button for the lift again with positive violence.

'I want a divorce…I'm not going to Italy!' she gasped stricken.

'You should have thought of that last night.' He stepped into the lift.

'It was a mistake!' she protested, unable even to lift her pounding head. 'Put me down…'

'You don't know what you're doing or saying,' Nico contended with tenacious determination, refusing even to meet her distressed gaze.

'I know…' She would have screamed the assurance had she had the strength. As it was, the amount of energy she had expended on frantic argument and the stress of her own emotional conflict had absolutely drained her. Nico's strong, dark features blurred as her weighted eyelids lowered. 'I hate you,' she mumbled hoarsely.

She drifted in and out of awareness from that point, too utterly wretched to consider anything but her own physical misery. Nico carried her on to the jet, wrapped in a blanket, and a while later she surfaced to hear a vaguely familiar voice sigh, 'The poor thing. I feel so sorry for her,' with a kind of oozing insincerity that grated on her hearing.

She recognized the stewardess, sultry wine-tinted mouth to the fore as she passed Nico a glass. As Nico lifted Gloria and tilted the contents of the glass to her mouth, she said, 'She hopes it's fatal.'

'Drink; it'll make you feel better,' Nico urged.

Nothing would. Bitterness surrounded Gloria. Nico had taken cruel advantage of her illness. Was nothing untouchable? As another shiver racked her aching body and she drank the noxious liquid because she knew that argument was futile, she looked up at him with condemning sapphire eyes. An act which ran little short of kidnapping was inexcusable.

'I couldn't leave you alone in a hotel in this condition,' Nico murmured as if she had spoken out loud.

'I'll never forgive you,' Gloria mumbled. 'I hope you catch it!'

Unexpectedly he laughed, the arm cradled round her shoulders curving her close in an obvious challenging of contagion which didn't surprise her. Nico was never ill. The very idea amused him. He had a godlike faith in his own robust health.

Her impressions became increasingly more fleeting from that point on. She lost her sense of time, her ability to distinguish between waking and sleeping. Had she been sleeping? She wondered when her eyes took in the crowds milling around them.

A fleeting exchange of Italy told her that they must have landed. It was the airport, she decided bitterly, and shut her eyes again, engulfed by a drowning sense of failure.

A sharp exchange of voices dragged her back to awareness. She was laid down on something, the blanket removed, a thermometer thrust into her dry mouth. Her heavy eyelids lifted on a white ceiling.

Not an airport, a hospital, she decided. She could hear Nico talking. He sounded angry, upset, and the other voice, which had been equally angry, was suddenly soft, soothing...a richly expressive, very female voice. With an enormous effort, Gloria turned her head to one side.

A woman in a white coat stood in the circle of Nico's arms. With one slim hand she was smoothing his black hair, caressing his hard jawline, and even as Gloria looked, she was reaching up to kiss him. Her lashes dropped again in shock.

The thermometer was removed...soon afterwards, a long time afterwards? She was sliding in and out of awareness. The next time she opened her eyes the woman was giving something to Nico, and she saw her properly.

The superb oval of her classically beautiful face below her crown of glossy black hair, the creamy skin and the great dark eyes brimming with so much warmth as they rested on Nico. A dry cough jolted through Gloria and both heads spun round.

Nico moved first. 'I thought you were asleep. This is Dr. Costello'

'Elena,' his companion inserted with an air of rather forced informality as she regarded Gloria with cool, professional distance. 'I am afraid that you will feel worse before you feel better, Gloria.'

Gloria closed her eyes, shutting them out in self-defense. She already felt a hundred times worse. She could feel her crumpled clothes, shiny, perspiring face and limp, damp hair. Her very bones were hurting. She wanted to cry but she didn't have the energy. Dear God, he brought me to his mistress for treatment; only Nico could be that cruel. Never in her life had Gloria felt more savaged.

'I was really scared,' Nico muttered roughly as he carried her somewhere. 'You looked so ill. I thought it might be pneumonia or something. And I didn't know what to do and I panicked.'

Panicked? Nico? It was an unlikely image in Gloria's disorientated mind. Then he was talking to someone in Italian, yet another female, this one younger, warmer, less controlled. Gloria was dimly aware of what sounded like a pretty heated argument and then she drifted off again, too wretched to care what was happening to her or around her.

There was a rushing sound somewhere in the background. Gloria's memory banks produced a jumbled mass of images and feelings. She had had a fever. She had gone from perspiring, shivering misery into the heat of what had felt like hell, with a whirling Catherine wheel of pain behind her temples. Day and night had merged indistinguishably.

She remembered being sponged down repeatedly and being so weak that even speaking was beyond her. She remembered Nico, silhouetted against the lamplit darkness of an unfamiliar room, Nico, hunched in a seat, oddly grey-looking in the dawn light. There had been other people too, but it felt like too much effort to remember them.

Her eyes opened. A maid was drawing curtains back on a spectacular wall of glass through which Gloria could see a slice of cloudless, densely blue sky. Then the sunlight blinded her, and she turned her head away, gratefully recognizing that her throat didn't hurt, her head didn't ache, and her muscles no longer protested every movement. The door closed. A sudden pressing need for the bathroom assailed her.

She attempted to sit up. Her body was disobedient. With a moan of impatience, she rolled her legs off the edge of the divan and slid down in an ungraceful heap on to the mercifully thick, deep pile of the carpet. It was a vast room. Lamplight had confusingly shrunk its contours.

Using the bed as a brace, she pushed herself upright and swayed like a drunk, registering that she was not quite as recovered as she had fondly imagined. But obstinacy got her to the suite.

An accidental meeting with her own reflection in a mirror horrified her. Who was that white scarecrow with the lank hank of hair? Fighting her own weakness, she knelt beside the bath to turn on the taps. At least if she was clean, she would feel better.

'Cristo! What the hell do you think you are doing?'

Gloria flinched and clutched the side of the bath. Nico towered over her, intimidatingly tall and dark. He looked tremendously elegant in a fabulously well-cut cream suit which merely accentuated his exotic coloring.

'Are you crazy?' he thundered, not content with having frightened her half out of her wits. 'You should be in bed!'

'I want a bath.' Gloria rested her cheek dully down on the cold ceramic edge, weak as a kitten. Then it came to her... Like a slow-motion replay from some distant dream, she saw him with Elena Castelo again.

Her heart seemed to stop beating. A chill like an icy winter wind enclosed her shrinking flesh.

'A bath when you can't even stand up?' Nico derided as he bent down to lift her. Gloria burst into floods of tears, disconcerting him as much as herself. But she had had no warning, no chance to stem those tears. They simply gushed forth as though someone had thrown an overload switch and forced their release. The effect on Nico was little short of staggering.

With a stifled imprecation in Italian, he scooped her up and cradled her while he apologized profusely for upsetting her and assured her that of course she could have a bath if she wanted one that badly.

It was just that she had been so ill, he stressed, and he was naturally afraid that she would over-exert herself and suffer a relapse. It was Nico metaphorically on his knees, Nico as she had never known him.

Ten minutes later, Gloria slid into her bath, and had not the image of the beautiful doctor still been lingering she might almost have been touched by the amount of concern Nico was displaying.

As it was, she simply didn't understand and was still too weak to devote her low energy resources to the puzzling question of why Nico should have gone to such lengths to force her to come to Italy to put a front on a marriage that had never been anything other than a charade for both.

Washing her hair exhausted her. When she emerged from the bathroom, she made no objection to being carried back to bed by Nico, although she was amazed that he had waited with such patience for her.

'I can hear the sea,' she murmured, finally identifying that rushing sound as waves surging up on to a shore.

'Do you remember anything of the trip here?' Unreadable dark eyes rested on her.

'Nothing,' she sighed.

'We're not in Sicily. When you were ill, there was little point in taking you to my mother's home. So, I brought you here instead.'

'And where is here?'

'Palermo, a small island which my father purchased shortly before his death. The perfect place for you to recuperate,' Nico said smoothly.

'An island?' Gloria raised an uncertain hand to her damp brow, her physical weakness slowing up her ability to think, but the one thought that did cross her dazed mind was that she knew precious little about her husband of five years.

A smiling, dark-eyed maid provided an interruption by arriving with a breakfast tray. Gloria's empty stomach gave a tiny leap as she registered just how hungry she was. 'How long have I been here?' she asked.

'Two days'

'Two?'

A flying knock sounded on the door and a teenager in cerise cycle shorts and a cropped top, her long hair a mass of glossy black ringlets, erupted into the room with a wide grin. 'Great, you're feeling better...'

'Gloria, this is my niece, Anna.'

'Everyone calls me Annie,' the tiny brunette broke in cheerfully. 'I came to meet you at the airport, but you won't remember me. You were practically unconscious.'

'I remember your voice.' Gloria smiled. Annie's friendliness was infectious. Yet once again she suffered that feeling of almost embarrassing ignorance. Nico's niece. He could have a dozen for all she knew.

'Gloria has to rest, not be talked into a relapse,' Nico warned.

Annie reddened, obviously sensitive to any reference to her chatterbox tendencies.

'But I'd love to have some company.' Gloria shot Nico's hard profile a speaking glance of reproach.

'Great!' Annie put herself down casually on the foot of the bed. 'You know, I thought you'd be older, but then maybe you're older than you look! What age are you?'

'Annie...' Nico breathed.

'Twenty-two'

'You got married at seventeen?' Annie swiveled her eyes, whose expression was a combination of shock and fascination, across to her uncle. 'And you agreed with my parents that you think that is far too young for me to be seriously dating?' she demanded.

Registering the gathering storm in Nico's discomposed features and holding back her own sudden desire to laugh, Gloria found herself surging to the cheerful teenager's rescue. 'You speak marvelous English, Annie.'

'I go to school in England. I wish I'd known you in London,' she complained afresh. 'I would have visited and got to know you years ago... in spite of what everybody else said!'

Nico released his breath in a sudden hiss and addressed his niece in Italian. Annie stiffened, a rebellious expression tightening her pretty face as she bent her head. What had the Julianne family said about Nico's wife whom they had never met? Gloria could not help being curious.

'Don't let her tire you out,' Nico sighed, heading for the door.

'Men are really thick sometimes,' Annie muttered and then threw a comically dismayed look at Gloria.

'Aren't they just!' Gloria laughed, belatedly realizing how very depressed she had been feeling before Annie's arrival. It was the flu which had done that to her, she told herself.

'I had to twist his arm to get to come here with you,' Annie confided. 'Nico always feels sorry for me because I have such a drag of a time when I'm home between terms.'

'I suppose all your friends are in England,' Gloria said.

'Oh, it's not that, it's the family being so old.' Annie scowled. 'They're all living in the last century!'

'Your parents?' Gloria was trying not to smile.

'Well, they're the youngest, I guess,' the teenager conceded bitterly. 'Only early fifties.'

'The youngest? Nico's only thirty...your mother, his sister, is that much older?'

'And her two sisters are older again. My grandmother is well into her seventies.'

Nico must have been a very late baby. Gloria found herself having to rearrange her assumptions. For some reason she had assumed that

Nico was the eldest child, not the youngest. It was rather unusual to have a gap of over twenty years between children, she thought absently.

'If only I'd known what you were like sooner,' Annie was still sad. 'I was so madly curious about you, too.'

'Is that why you came to meet us at the airport?' Gloria smiled again.

'No, that was because I wanted you to know how welcome you were. I think the way my family have treated you is horrible,' Annie said very earnestly.

Gloria sipped her coffee. 'And you were the exact same age as I am now,' the teenager continued heatedly as she sprang off the bed and wandered over to the window.

'I know how I would feel if my husband's family refused to have anything to do with me...I'd be very hurt and then I'd get furious!'

Illumination sank in on Gloria. The Julianne family had evidently rejected her sight unseen. Nico had not deliberately excluded her from his family circle. But Gloria felt neither hurt nor furious. Theirs had not been a normal marriage. She had had more to worry about than the uninterest of Nico's distant family, although she was suddenly distinctly grateful not to be a guest in her mother-in-law's house.

'I'm not furious,' she said wryly.

'But it was so unfair. It wasn't your fault that Nico fell madly in love with you and backed out of his engagement with Elena Castelo !' Annie scowled impressively in the pin-dropping silence. 'I mean, that was just one of those things and it would have been a lot worse if he'd fallen for you after he'd married her. Don't you think?'

Graciously, Gloria was saved from the necessity of a reply as a maid entered and addressed Annie.

'Rats! Mother on the phone,' the teenager groaned, and then grinned. 'She won't ask any questions, I bet, but she must be just gasping to know all about you! She's terribly fond of Nico.' She frowned, noticing Gloria. 'I'll see you later.'

'Lovely,' Gloria said shakily, flying on automatic pilot after a revelation which had literally depth-charged her out of her weak dreaminess. She tasted blood in her mouth, registered that she had bitten down painfully on her tongue to prevent a shocked exclamation escaping her. Well, well, well, she thought, struggling manfully to recover from the shock.

Chapter 18

Nico's Secret

Gloria was shattered. Five years ago, they had been engaged to be married. Evidently Nico might not have been hostile to a little romance, but he had already had his future wife lined up. At least he had, Gloria adjusted, until her father had pleaded to a change of bride. Gloria felt sick as the full meaning of what she had learned.

Nico and Elena Costello were lovers. So why had Nico insisted that Gloria remain his wife? Why had he refused to snatch at his freedom? Didn't he want to marry Elena? Or was he quite content to retain the good doctor as his mistress, his demonstrably devoted mistress, who couldn't even keep her paws off him in the presence of his wife?

Gloria shuddered; she believed that there was nothing in the Hippocratic oath that prohibited such behavior. No wonder Nico had been so bitter about their marriage! Nico had not chosen to tell her the whole truth of what their marriage had cost him.

On the other hand, Nico was certainly beginning to settle the score for what he had suffered. Could that possibly be mere coincidence? Dear God, Nico had to hate her! It was a nonsense surely for him to say that he did not.

More miserable, more isolated than she had ever felt in her life before, Gloria buried her aching head in the pillows. Just as Mike had manipulated Nico and forcibly rearranged his life five years ago, Nico was now bringing to bear a similar pressure on Mike's daughter.

Nico had first revealed what might have been called a 'sudden' attraction towards his previously invisible wife the day Gloria had told him she was in love with another man. Before that, he had believed that she still loved him and no doubt over the years he had reaped a sympathetic satisfaction from punishing her for her father's sins by demonstrating his complete indifference towards her.

He didn't yet know that Paul was out of her life, but he had been ruthlessly determined to achieve that end. Why? An eye for an eye, a tooth for a tooth? Nico had been robbed of Elena five years ago. Was he intent on putting Gloria through the same torment of losing a loved one? Was he capable of being that brutal?

Her father was out of reach, had been out of reach of any form of revenge even while alive by virtue of his blackmail, but Gloria was very much within reach and always had been.

Yes, Nico could be cruel. She remembered his cruel self-assurance that even Mike couldn't force him to perform like a stud in her bed. Her pounding head was whirling. She thought back shrinkingly to Nico's passionate possession of her, only now recalled his unashamed admission that that had been a deliberate trick.

At the time she had believed that he meant he had slept with her both to reinforce his belief that they could have a real marriage and to tear a gaping hole in her confident statement that she loved Paul even to punish her for daring to confront him.

Only now did she see another, even more humiliating explanation for that night. A turn of the screw, a heightening of the victim's torment Nico, with all his considerable sexual savoir-faire, setting out with cool calculation to seduce his wife and thus throw her into absolute turmoil.

Suddenly she felt painfully degraded by her own weakness in his arms, the unsuspected vulnerability which had made her a pushover for all that smoldering, sizzling Italian machismo. Nico had just loved that discovery. The awareness was like a knife twisting in an open wound.

Exhaustion sent her into an uneasy sleep from which she awoke to find that it was after midnight. She had slept solid for more than twelve hours. Evidently it had done her good. Physically she was feeling much stronger even if she did feel as though she was on the point of starvation.

Pulling on a light robe, she went off in search of food. Her mind was filled with all the frightening thoughts she had suffered earlier and, preoccupied as she was, she got the shock of her life when Nico appeared silently in a doorway just as she was passing.

A whisper of unformed sound ejected from her lips, and she backed away in a hurry, her shoulder-blades colliding with the cold stone wall on the other side of the passageway.

'Looking for a phone?'

In the dim light, his striking features might have been a bronze sculpture, eyes a mere sliver of black below the dark curves of his lashes.

Gloria pressed a helpless hand to the wild thump of her heartbeat. 'A phone...?' she stammered blankly.

'Judging by the length of your calls to Woods, you were heavily into the substitute of telephone sex,' Nico murmured with silken insolence. 'And you've had forty-eight hours at least without your daily fix.

Well, if that is what it takes, never let it be said that I shrank from the challenge. Go back to your room and I'll use the internal line because I promise you anything he can do I can do better...'

Gloria sucked in air in a whoosh, infuriatingly shattered by the smooth suggestion. 'You pervert!'

Nico groaned. 'It goes against the grain, but I'm beginning to pity your blond lover. He had what? Two and a half months? What did you do with him? Hold hands, sigh, and share deeply meaningful conversations?'

Red as a beet now and simmering, Gloria's teeth gritted. 'None of your business!'

'But you see me here...' Nico spread expressive brown hands in a movement that deliberately betrayed his savage amusement ' enslaved by my need to know every gory detail.'

Trembling with rage, Gloria turned on her heel. 'I'm hungry,' she said in a frigid voice.

'Not for him, you weren't. Maybe you were hungry for a little attention and romance. I can understand that' Nico drawled in the tone of one attempting to hold a deeply meaningful conversation and struggling.

'You're so arrogance with which he talked down to her.

'At least I'm trying to understand what attracted you to a third-rate wimp like Woods!' he slammed back at her in a devastatingly sudden explosion of raw anger.

'I've got very bad taste, Nico. Don't you know that? After all, once I chose you.'

Adrenalin was racing through Gloria's veins. She saw something in Nico which she had not seen before and wondered that she had been so blind.

Nico was not jealous of Paul no, that would have been far too exaggerated a description of what he was feeling right now. It undoubtedly offended Nico's macho pride to believe that his wife preferred another man to him. Right at that moment it would have killed Gloria to admit that Paul was yesterday's news and as third-rate as Nico had claimed.

His brilliant eyes glittered over her, and she could feel the raw force of his powerful personality beating down on her. It was oddly exhilarating, not demeaning, as that little scene with the towel had been that day in Paris when Nico had fondly imagined that all he had to do was crook an arrogant finger and she would do what he wanted... willingly, eagerly, gratefully... the way all the other women had in Nico's capricious existence.

'You need' Nico began.

'Well, I don't need half my clothes ripped off me like the last time,' Gloria cut in, lifting her chin high and shooting him a look of splendid mockery.

The silence lay there, thick, and impenetrable, disturbed only by the thump of her own heartbeat in her ears.

For a split-second Nico stared at her with black eyes as dense as the night and then his sensual mouth gave a sudden appreciative twist, and he threw back his dark head and burst out laughing. Sharply disconcerted, Gloria stared back at him, color flooding her cheeks. Without warning, she felt very weak.

As she made a hurried movement to walk away, he caught her back with a powerful hand and guided her into the room he had recently vacated. 'You said you were hungry. I'll order some food,' he said, abruptly dull.

Not a dull man, she reflected as she was thrust down abruptly on a comfortable sofa across from the cluttered desk he had clearly been working at. She linked her not quite steady hands, ruefully conscious of the internal upheaval that resulted from being in Nico's range.

You never knew what was likely to happen next. Once that had fascinated her. He was so different from her. They were night and day, chalk, and cheese. And yet when he had laughed, she had been made shatteringly aware of the electrifying charisma that was so innate a part of him.

Why should she be surprised by that? Why should she feel threatened by that acknowledgement? Nico was devastatingly good-looking, sexy, very sexy. He couldn't help being like that. She had watched him at dinner parties, the effortless cynosure of all female attention. He took it for granted. It had always been that way for Nico, she imagined.

His mother and sisters probably worshipped the ground he walked on too. So really it was only natural that she should also be aware of that natural magnetism, should find momentarily that the ground lurched almost dizzily beneath her on receipt of one dazzling smile.

Yes, it was only natural, wasn't it? It didn't mean anything, just that she was female and alive. 'I'm glad that you are feeling stronger, but you look very serious,' Nico drawled.

Gloria took a deep breath. As she glanced up, she caught the dancing remnants of humor in his clear gaze and her mouth ran dry. Nico in charm mode—well, that was a new one to her, wasn't it? Deliberately she fixed her gaze to one side of him. 'We need to talk.' Nico laughed softly. ' It is too late.'

Her husband, the chauvinist pig. Any minute now he'd be telling her not to worry her little head about anything. Nico, she appreciated with a stab of pain, had never taken her seriously. Maybe he never took any woman seriously or maybe it was because she was small and blonde and once, she had been crazy about him and he knew it.

Five years ago, Nico had put her on ice. He had left her to exist in limbo, neither free nor married. In that interim it had not occurred to him that her feelings might have changed. He had not been interested in her feelings. He had been far too bound up in furious resentment and bitterness even to spare a thought for what she might be suffering.

It had not occurred to him that she might turn to another man. It had not occurred to him that she might be willing to sacrifice the financially privileged lifestyle that being a Julianne gave her to gain her freedom. Nico had falsely assumed that the money and the status were very important to her. Those were the barriers she had to breach.

'Nico, we have to talk, and, if it's possible, without you getting angry, threatening or sarcastic,' Gloria murmured tightly.

Nico was lounging back against the edge of his desk, surveying her with an air of maddening indulgence, the same way that one might look at a child struggling to be amusingly mature beyond its years. Yet, she could sense tension within him on another level.

'Nico'

'Your meal.' At spectacular speed, Nico strode across the room and whipped a tray from a dumbstruck manservant. It was equally astonished. Had it been anyone else but Nico, who had all the sensitivity of a beating-ram, she would have thought he was being deliberately misleading.

'Eat.' The tray was placed on her lap.

'Nico, I know about you and Elena .'

He swung back to her, a frown-line pleating his winged ebony brows. 'Annie,' he guessed grimly. 'What do you know?'

'I understand that you were engaged to her.'

'For years,' Nico admitted with baffling casualness.

Gloria looked at her exquisitely arranged salad with sinking appetite and lifted the silverware. 'Well, I can understand how you must have felt when Mike put you in a position where you had to break that engagement and lose the woman you loved.'

'The timing was inconvenient...'

Gloria lifted her head. 'Inconvenient?' she echoed half an octave higher.

Nico released his breath with impatience. 'I have known Elena all my life. We were promised in our teens. The decision had nothing to do with us. It was what our fathers wanted, a merger between two shipping lines.

Elena wanted to be a doctor. Her father did not approve but my support brought him around. Both Elena and I knew that eventually we would have to disappoint our families but in the interim, it suited both of us to play along.'

'Play along?' Gloria questioned.

'If I had said that I did not wish to marry Elena her father would have pressured her to marry someone else and she might never have got to study medicine,' Nico explained, his mouth twisting.

'You must understand that Elena is a dedicated doctor who gives virtually one hundred per cent to her vocation. She has time for little else. She is not the wife I would have chosen for myself, nor was I the husband she would have chosen...'

Gloria swallowed hard, trying to absorb his calm promise and tie it in with what she had believed she had seen in that hospital. Close friends embracing? Elena had been so loving towards Nico but then people who had known each other all their lives inclined to be and possibly it had been some time since they had last met, Gloria reasoned uncertainly under the attack of Nico's level inquiry. His cool candor was impressive, she had to admit.

'You weren't in love with her?'

'I believed I was once.' Nico smiled with ironic recall. 'But I was only eighteen. Elena was beautiful. That was all that mattered. It was not very long before her concentration in her studies made me see that we were incompatible.'

'You wanted her one hundred per cent vocation to be targeted on you.'

'You know me so well.'

'Frankly, it was just an observation,' Gloria said stiffly. 'Why did you call the timing of our marriage inconvenient?'

'Elena's father blamed my defection on her dedication to her career and she was forced into open conflict with her family before she had won her independence.'

'And how did your family react?' Gloria heard herself prompt tightly.

'With shock, horror and shame at my behavior,' Nico numbered flatly. 'A promise is a serious commitment in the Italian society, most particularly to a family as immersed in traditional beliefs as mine. I was accused of dishonoring the Julianne's name. It is true that inevitably the engagement would have been broken but the fact that I immediately married someone else magnified the offence in their eyes.'

Gloria studied the carpet and she saw her father like a cold force at the center of a storm, carrying the elements within his grasp without caring about the damage he inflicted. 'I'm sorry,' she sighed.

'It's immaterial now. Last year Elena married another doctor.' Nico's strong features tightened. 'Both families were satisfied by that development. If they do not concede that we had a right to choose our own partners, I do believe they both acknowledge that Elena and I would not have been suited.'

Gloria began picking on her salad, a little embarrassed at her dramatic assumption that Elena was Nico's mistress. A newly married woman, a lifelong friend. Why should she not have openly demonstrated her fondness for Nico?

Perhaps she had misinterpreted what she saw because she had never been able to offer anyone that kind of affection. Her father hadn't wanted it. Nico hadn't wanted it. By the time Paul came along, she had been prevented by the habit of concealing her emotions.

The silence remained. Deep in thought, Gloria ate her meal.

'You close me out as if I'm invisible,' Nico murmured silkily. 'When you do that, I want to smash things and shout.'

Her silvery head flew up, glaring confusion engraved in her sapphire eyes. 'That's childish.'

Nico shrugged a broad shoulder with magnificent unconcern. 'There is a child inside every one of us.'

Gloria cleared her throat awkwardly, strangely disconcerted by that unexpected admission and the ease with which he'd made it. Living with Nico, she decided, was like camping out on the side of a live volcano. There was always a rumble, a warning quake of suggested disaster in the air.

'Why won't you let me go?' she demanded starkly.

'You're my wife.'

'Not good enough.'

Nico spread beautifully shaped fingers. 'That certificate is still out there,' he reminded her drily.

Gloria paled. 'But my father is dead...he probably destroyed it!'

'He destroyed nothing else,' Nico pointed out. ' Mike was very clever. I may have despised him but even I must acknowledge that. Who knows what he might have arranged? If we split up, if we part, somebody somewhere may be primed to use that certificate to hurt my family.'

'That's being paranoid!' Gloria whispered unevenly, her head beginning to ache.

'It's not a risk I am prepared to take. As far as Mike was concerned, you were content to be my wife right up until the day he died,' Nico said smoothly. 'He knew no different. I believe that he would have taken a special pleasure from confirming that if I ever attempted to divorce you, I would pay.'

The most obvious explanation had evaded her, she conceded numbly, her hands clenching tightly together. She had let her imagination run riot. She had believed that Nico might well be punishing her for her father's sins. She had believed that Paul's very existence so outraged Nico's pride that he was set on hanging on to her out of pure dog-in-the-manger bloody-mindedness.

She had even begun to believe that based on practical, unemotional reasoning he might indeed consider her to be a suitable wife. The terrible reality was that every one of those motivations had been considerably nicer to her ego than the awful truth she had finally been forced to acknowledge.

Nico thought he was stuck with her for eternity like a burden. If he hadn't been so accustomed to being in that position, he might well have been wondering whether a suitably organized accident might not best meet his requirements.

'You've turned a little...pale,' he mused.

'I've got a headache,' Gloria stuttered.

She was remembering the fury which had brought him to her hotel, a fury which she now saw had been entirely divorced from any personal feelings on his side.

After all, Nico couldn't allow her to leave him. Even if he really wanted to throw the door wide and encourage her to leave, he couldn't risk doing it. Marrying her had indeed been the life sentence he had called it.

For the first time she understood how furiously helpless he must have felt in the grip of that awareness early on in their marriage and how desperately he must have hoped that she would meet and fall for someone else while her father was still alive, thereby releasing him from the union.

After all, had that been her choice, Mike could scarcely have blamed Nico. No wonder he had left her alone for five years and no wonder he had accused her in Paris of being obscenely faithful and loyal. Why had she chosen not to examine that condemnation more closely? Why had she buried it?

The tray was removed. Nico bent down and began to lift her. 'I can manage!' she gasped stricken, but he ignored her. Settled back on the bed, Gloria snatched at the sheet and turned over on her stomach, unable even to look at him. She felt stripped of every ounce of pride, every inch of dignity. She was drowning in humiliation.

In a couple of minutes, Nico had changed everything. What right did she have to demand her freedom now? Whether she liked it or not, it had been her infatuation with Nico which had trapped him into this situation. Even Mike wouldn't have tried to push her into marriage with a man she neither wanted nor loved.

'You'd feel more comfortable without that robe.'

Gloria tensed, having been unaware that he was still in the room.

'It doesn't matter.'

'You need a good night's sleep.'

She felt the sheet move, hands at her waist, gently tugging loose the sash and then sliding the robe down off her shoulders to remove it. The sheet was smoothed back into place.

Nico sighed softly. 'You know this is my bedroom. Would you mind very much if I moved back in?'

Gloria went rigid and then quivered. 'I'll move now,' she managed, beginning to lift her head.

'I want you to stay,' he breathed in a curiously stifled tone.

'Oh...' Gloria froze, violently disturbed by the announcement.

'We are married,' he murmured.

The silence stretched, biting at her every nerve-ending.

'Yes.' It was a whisper so faint that the sound of a pin dropping would have been louder. It was an acknowledgement which Gloria had avoided, protested, and denied for years. Now it had been forced on her.

She lay there in shock. There was no other word to describe her condition. The durable foundations of her resentment and bitterness and her determination to leave him had been blown to pieces and right now she was still lying in the bomb crater, fumbling feebly to find some reasonable excuse for denying him the right to sleep in his own bed and the expectation that she share that same bed. The truth was that there wasn't any reasonable excuse available to her.

Nico had come to terms with their future that day in Paris. She saw that now. He had got to the bottom of that safety-deposit box and emerged without the ticket to freedom he had vainly sought. For a little while he had hoped that she had it. That wretched certificate that she had never even heard of before that day!

When he had realized that unpleasant reality, he had known simultaneously that their marriage was indeed a life sentence. Consequently, his sudden change of attitude towards her. If escape was out of the question, he had to make the best of imprisonment. If he could not free himself to marry another woman, he had to make the best of the one he had got...

Suddenly, Gloria was out of defenses. Hadn't she brought all of this on them both? Hadn't she, in her complete and utter stupidity, agreed to marry a man who had looked like death warmed up on the day he had proposed? She had asked him if he was ill. Ill?

Three weeks had passed before the wedding and she had only seen him twice in company and he had been so cool and so distant, he had been like a stranger. Had she smelt a rat? No way! She had been heading over heels in love and had told herself he was preoccupied with business.

A slight sound dredged her from her frantic lashings of self-loathing. She turned her head. Her lowered lashes swept up, revealing startled blue eyes. Nik was undressing. Tension thrumming through every tautened muscle, Leah closed her eyes again. But she listened, just as she listened minutes later to the sound of the shower running. Ordinary, everyday sounds for most married women only not for her. She found herself imagining the state of the bathroom. A heap of discarded wet towels and nothing used returned to its proper place.

She had a complete memory of having once invaded Nico's wing of the New York house after he had departed one morning. She remembered the wet towels, the disorder, and the disturbing, frightening realization that no two people could have been more separate or less intimate than they were in their marriage that was not a marriage.

After that she had felt like a tenant in his beautiful house. She had never stamped her personality anywhere, never moved a single piece of furniture. That day had been the beginning of her detachment from him. Just as this day had forever shattered that same protective device.

Her ears cut up in disbelief at the sound of Nico humming a brief snatch from a famous operatic aria out of tune. He sounded so cheerful. Her lashes lifted. She clashed unexpectedly with gleaming jet. Nico was standing by the bed gazing down at her. Instantly his gaze veiled, the curve of his expressive mouth straightening out.

'Go to sleep,' he instructed almost soothingly.

She closed her eyes, heard him discard the towel which was all that had interrupted her view of that lean, agile golden body. The mattress gave ever so slightly, the sheet slid and then the light went out.

Silence fell. Gloria lay as still as a corpse but considerably wider awake, knowing that she could not possibly sleep with Nico lying naked within a foot of her, his every uneasy movement filling her with instinctive alarm and rocketing tension.

Wonderfully warm and relaxed, Gloria gave a graceful little wriggle and the hard heat of the body next to hers squeezed. Her lashes lifted. She looked up into burning black eyes, fringed by ebony lashes. The impact of those eyes was captivating. Her blood leapt in her veins and her heat raced. She felt dizzy, breathless, and utterly dispossessed of all rational thought.

A fingertip stroked along the lush ripeness of her lower lip. 'Open your mouth for me. I want to taste you,' Nico urged huskily. Held fast by his searing gaze, she instinctively obeyed and with a muted groan of satisfaction he crushed her slender form to him, his hands sweeping over her hips and her back as his hard, demanding mouth took hers with savage intensity.

A sweet, twisting ache stirred in her belly. The tip of his tongue snaked between her readily parted lips, erotically probing the tender inner reaches to make her tremble with helpless excitement beneath him.

With insistent hands Nico tugged the thin straps of her nightdress down from her shoulders, baring the pouting swell of her breasts. His sure fingers cupped and explored the straining mounds and caressed her nipples until they were throbbing and stiff. Uncontrollably her hips arched up to his, her thighs trembling in response as her hands rose and tangled in his thick black hair.

Her heart hammered wildly in her chest as he released her reddened lips. He teased her exposed breasts, his tongue skimming down the valley between them while his hands toyed with the rigid peaks he had created.

Heat was surging through her in waves of violent response and when he employed his mouth on her tender flesh instead, she moaned low in her throat, subjected to a storm of exquisite sensation that tormented.

She was intoxicated, enslaved by passion, lost in a world of intense and drugging pleasure. With a soft growl of anticipation, Nico took her mouth again with compulsive hunger and pulled her against him, his hand sliding through the silvery curls at the top of her thighs, searching out the silken softness beneath with intimate expertise, each sensual invasion calculated to heighten the fevered and mindless response he was receiving.

It was a sweet agony of delight that made her sob and pant for breath. Her hips jerked and lifted of their own desire, the demanding ache of desire rising to an unbearable pitch. A whimper of frustration was torn from her. His hands sank beneath her as he slid between her thighs.

He threw back his head and raised her to meet the powerful thrust of his hard body. With an earthy groan of unashamed pleasure, he drove his rigid, swollen length into her soft depths.

Letting her body stretch to accommodate his raw invasion, the sensation still new enough to shock, and then he moved inside her, creating a greedy need that burned through her entire body.

Unconsciously her fingers dug into his smooth, muscular back, her breath sobbing in her throat with every urgent thrust. Joyous sensation took over as he possessed her so thoroughly that she was driven out of her mind with sheer, fragmenting pleasure. When release came it consumed her utterly for long, timeless moments and then dropped her down gently into sweet, drowning slowness.

'Heaven is said to come to he who waits,' Nico murmured silkily, curving her confidently into the damp, hot heat of him. 'But I was always a speculator and patience is not one of my virtues.'

Exhausted and satisfied, Gloria couldn't think straight, and while her mind was attempting to function again, she slid back into sleep. When she wakened again the curtains were wide, the sun high in the sky and a breakfast tray, its contents clotting now, lay on the cabinet on her side of the bed. She looked for Nico, but he was gone. Gloria felt sadness and alone.

It was midday but as she got out of bed, all that she could think about was the events around dawn. Her crumpled nightdress lay in a heap on the carpet like an accusing statement and a flush of shame flamed over her skin, a sigh of intense mortification dragged from her as she looked at the evidence in horror.

He had woken her up, he had deliberately woken her up out of a sound sleep and confirmed that she didn't have a chance to consider what she was doing! She washed herself from head to toe in the shower, but she couldn't wash away the intimate ache that reminded her of his lovemaking.

Why did she blame him? she asked herself abruptly. Why did she keep on kidding herself that he was the only one responsible for what happened every time he touched her?

The truth was that when Nico touched her, she melted, she burned, she craved with a reckless lack of control that was so obvious to her, it could scarcely be a revelation to him. Without the smallest effort, he had taught her to want him before she'd even known what she wanted.

Five years ago, that instinctive desire had made her uneasy, embarrassed, and unnatural in his presence. She hadn't been ready for that intensity and when Nico had left her to sleep alone it had been a relief to close out those disturbing sensations which had once afflicted her whenever he was close. When he had chosen to smash down that wall, she had put up in self-defense he had unleashed a flood of passion as powerful as a tidal wave.

She had never stopped wanting him any more than she had denied herself the ridiculous responsibility of buying his socks. The one personal thing she had ever done for him, and she had clung to it right to the bitter end.

God, it was so pitiful; little wonder he had laughed. Nico probably had more socks than Imelda Marcos had had shoes. Tears stood out in her anguished eyes as she saw inside herself.

Some rejected women clung, she had bought socks with the compulsion of a fetishist, fixed stupid flower arrangements in his wing of the house to remind him of her existence, turned herself slowly but surely from an unsophisticated teenager into one of the most elegant women in New York. There wasn't a bit of her she hadn't made over for his benefit. It was pathetic to love a man so blindly utterly, unforgivably pathetic.

She did love him. She had fought that love with Paul and denied its existence, unconsciously fighting for the freedom that her pride demanded. Nothing had changed. Nico didn't love her, never would love her. He was just stuck with her.

On his side, the sex was merely...merely functional. He woke up in bed with a female body and what happened next was one of the very few things that was entirely predictable about Nico.

So, she needn't start telling herself that her husband had suddenly begun to find her an unbearable temptation. Nico was a very manly male, and he wasn't given to soul-searching over something as basic as his sexual needs.

He wouldn't let her go unless that certificate turned up and for the very first time Gloria was consumed by a need to know more. Was it a marriage certificate, a birth certificate, a share certificate...? Faintly she enumerated several more possibilities. The first two were unlikely, she decided.

Nico had said he was protecting his family. He had never mentioned himself, so had someone committed some sort of crime in his family? Embezzlement, financial dishonesty?

Wrapped in a cleverly cut blue dress, she walked out on to the wide terrace that overlooked the sea and the cliffs far below. In any other mood, she would have wanted to take in the spectacular view and explore the rest of the house but her sole driving compulsion was to find Nico.

He was standing on the terrace, dark and lean and flexible in tailored cream chinos and an open-necked black shirt. As he heard her steps, his dark head turned. She hesitated under the full assault of his night-dark eyes, indeed was so wildly disorientated that she very nearly cannoned into a lounger nearby.

Color flooded her cheeks, an aching, terrifying awareness trembling through her slender form. She couldn't take her eyes off his starkly handsome golden features and was plunged into instant recall of how she had felt in his arms hours earlier.

He dealt her a dazzling smile and strode fluidly towards her. 'How do you feel?'

'Fine...'

'Just fine... You look spectacular,' he murmured with a slightly ragged edge to his deep, dark voice. His eyes ran over her in a blatantly possessive scrutiny, taking in the fall of silvery hair, the delicate perfection of her glowing face, and roamed right on down to her toes, taking unashamed note of every curve he found in route. 'Glorious,' he added, reaching for both her hands, and drawing her close.

Her heart pounded and she tried to steady it, confusion in her sapphire eyes. 'Nico.'

Everything she had intended to say went straight back out of her head again.

'Am I interrupting something?' Annie asked chirpily, causing both their heads to spin round.

'Not at all.' Nico smiled, releasing Gloria's hands just as she attempted to snatch them away.

'The staff are hovering with lunch,' Annie explained, watching Nico swing out a chair by the table and settle Gloria into it.

Gloria was conscious that her hands were shaking. The full effect of Nico's warmth and admiration had shaken her. It couldn't mean anything. Maybe he was always charm personified with a new lover. For that was really all she was. New, fresh, different in every way from the women he usually took to his bed. The charm wouldn't last. Women bored Nico easily and quickly. She had always known that.

Lunch was served. Annie chattered about inconsequential things. Every time Gloria looked up from her plate she was entrapped by Nico's slumbrous gaze, and her pulse would quicken, and her temperature would rise, making her reach for her wine with increasing regularity.

Nico's mobile phone buzzed. He left the table to pick it up where it lay on a chair several yards away.

'I can't wait until the rest of the family see this,' Annie chuckled.

'Sorry, I...?' Gloria dragged her attention from N's vibrant smile in her direction as he talked into the phone. It was no mean accomplishment.

'You're locked into each other like a pair of magnets on a honeymoon. When I invited myself along, I had no idea what I was getting into!' Annie grinned to show that she wasn't offended. 'I'm going swimming. I'll see you later.'

Hot-cheeked, Gloria bent her head. She grabbed up her wine again. It gave her something to do with her hands. She had come out here to talk seriously to Nico, a challenge at the best of times but a positively mountainous challenge when, for the very first time in five years, he was treating her like a highly desirable woman and being shatteringly attentive.

Draining her glass, she stood. Nico curved his arms around her from behind, taking her by surprise. As he tugged her relentlessly back into contact with the abrasively masculine angles of his powerful form her dangerous body trembled with an instantaneous response which terrified her, and she tensed.

'What's wrong?' he breathed from above her head.

'There's something we need to discuss.'

'Forget it. If the discussion is likely to harbor a single mention of divorce, separation, sexual abstention, or Woods, let me give you a hint,' he said with sudden harshness. 'Keep your mouth closed.'

An entirely unexpected spurt of amusement attacked her. He always thought he was one step ahead of her and for once he wasn't. 'It's not about any of those things.'

Nico tugged her around. 'Then it's not important.'

Before she had even guessed his intention, he was covering her mouth hungrily with his own. It was heavier than the wine she tasted on his lips, sweeter than anything she had ever known.

Helplessly she leaned into him, snaking her arms round his neck to stay upright, the flames of her response burning up every skin cell. His fingers splayed beneath the curve of her hips, lifting her into electrifying contact with the unmistakable thrust of his erection.

'I want you again,' he muttered thickly.

She wanted him so badly there was an ache low in the pit of her stomach, her mind suddenly a shameful receptacle for erotic images that were shatteringly new to her experience. The very strength of the passion he could remind within her devastated her.

He didn't even have to use pretty words or compliments. He didn't even have to try. A few kisses and she simply fired into spontaneous combustion. Like a sex toy, a submissive little doll that he could manipulate entirely to the dictates of his own needs. That image gave her the strength to pull back from him.

'I have to talk to you,' she framed, and turned towards the house. 'And I think we should go inside.'

'We can talk in bed.' Nico tracked her with greedy black eyes.

'You only got out of bed a few hours ago!' Gloria heard herself hiss.

' I can't wait to get back there.'

How did you switch him off again? she wondered wildly, dismally conscious of the tension of her nipples and the tingling heat deep in the very heart of her. It occurred to her that if she was programmed for his benefit he was very much programmed on the same wavelength and that if she relaxed her guard for one tiny second, he was intent on taking advantage of that.

'I think you're over-sexed,' she whispered, sharply displeased by what was happening between them.

'You're complaining?' He dealt her a blazing smile.

Gloria achieved the cool of what appeared to be the main reception-room, perspiration beading her short upper lip. She sank down on a sofa. 'That's so cute! Your feet don't touch the floor!' Nico laughed and, instead of picking another seat as she had hoped, crouched down in front of her. 'So, talk,' he invited, studying her with heavy-lidded eyes.

'It's not impossible.' Gloria was becoming uncomfortable although she could understand Annie's curiosity. Her request for an explanation of what she had overheard at eleven had obviously been greeted with maternal dismay and distress and a brick wall of silence. She was a lively, intelligent girl, still clearly troubled by the response she had received.

Annie shrugged. 'The secrecy must have made it much harder for Nico.'

'People are much more open about adoption now than they were thirty years ago.' Gloria took a deep breath. 'But we shouldn't be talking about this, Annie. It's too private and, before you ask me, no, I don't know anything more than you do.'

Annie went a fierce red and bent her head. 'I'm sorry. I don't know why I brought it up.'

'Because I'm family and yet not family,' Gloria supplied gently. 'I think you have to accept that Nico has a right to privacy about something that personal and I may be wrong, but I doubt that it would be a good idea to raise the subject with him.'

'I wouldn't dream of it.' Annie was horrified at the idea.

Gloria smoothly changed the subject and hoped she had firmly dissuaded the younger girl from further indiscreet questioning. Long after Annie had said goodnight Gloria was bothered by what she had been told.

In some ways she knew nothing about Nico and that hurt; no matter how unreasonable that was, it hurt. She wandered into the drawing-room where she had noticed the magnificent grand piano earlier in the day and sat down on the stool.

So, Nico was an adopted. It was foolish to feel hurt that he had never even made a fleeting mention of the fact. After all, it was obvious that his family had gone to some lengths to conceal the adoption.

His parents had had three daughters and must have badly wanted a son. In a veil of secrecy, they had adopted a baby boy. Over the years Gloria had read several profiles on Nico in the newspapers and not one of them had referred to that. Annie was right. Nobody outside the family circle knew.

What age was Nico before he learned the truth? Had his parents been more honest in private than they had been in public? If they hadn't been, it must have been one hell of a shock, she reflected, her fingers moving nimbly over the gleaming keyboard, the rich brilliance of a Chopin concerto flooding the room with the music she often employed to accompany her deepest thoughts.

She hoped Annie had the sense to be discreet. Some secrets you just had to live with. Maybe Nico didn't want anybody to know either. Or maybe he simply didn't care, considered it scarcely relevant to his adult life.

He was very attached to the family she had yet to meet. He was capable of very strong emotions. Why had she never seen that before? A male capable of marrying a woman he didn't love merely to protect his family was a male capable of putting other people's needs ahead of his own. Although it was a little hard to appreciate his sacrifice when she had been part of the burnt offering.

Dear God, she thought, with a surge of sudden pain, how could she exist in a marriage where nothing was given or shared but a bed? It was too late for her to accept that. Maybe years ago, when she hadn't known any better, hadn't known Nico for the man that he was, she would have happily settled for what he was prepared to give her, but not now, when every sense craved more.

She had no choice, and even if she did have a choice, did she really have the strength to walk away from him? Was half a loaf better than no bread? She lifted her hands from the keyboard in sudden bitter distress.

'Don't stop...'

Her spine rigid, Leah slowly swiveled round on the stool. Nico was standing in the shadows by the window. A shimmering tension emanated from the tautness of his stance; his black eyes glittered in his dark face. His hair was tousled, his shirt half unbuttoned, his jawline blue-shadowed.

'Play for me,' he said roughly, and it was not a request.

Gloria spun back round to the piano. Her sapphire eyes flared. She lifted her slim hands and played 'Chopsticks', every deliberately discordant note expressing her mood of defiance.

A set of hard fingers closed round her narrow wrists and jerked them up. Sudden silence spread through the room, broken only by her own fractured breathing. She could feel the warmth of his powerful body, raw with tension, mere inches from her as he bent over her. A shiver ran through her.

'Why?' he grated, releasing her wrists.

'I'm not your slave,' she muttered shakily, but that wasn't why. She remembered playing for him years ago, remembered that first night; she had never played for him since. Music had always been her mode of self-expression. It had become far too personal to share with Nico.

'Play,' he said again.

Her hands were trembling. The atmosphere was dangerously charged with every forceful element of Nik's volatile temperament.

'I have no music.'

'You can play for hours without music,' he reminded her harshly.

Fatigued by his loving presence, she began to play, snatches of this, pieces of that, but her usually nimble fingers were reluctant to do her bidding smoothly and several jarring notes disturbed the performance. After the fourth mistake her fingers slid from the keyboard.

'You're very stubborn. I should have realized that' Nico breathed. 'You may look as fragile as spun glass but you're not.'

Right now, Gloria felt very fragile. Every nerve-ending was singing with the high-wire tension in the room. Slowly she stood up, reluctant to look anywhere near him.

'So, tell me about him,' he invited dangerously quietly.

Her head spun round, silver hair flying back from her delicate cheekbones. He had cut off her intended exit route. 'I don't know what.'

'Your lover...' Eyes dark as an abyss rested on her expectantly.

A frisson of alarm snaked through her. 'You can't possibly want to hear about Paul.'

'Can't I?' Nico challenged, treating her to a lethal smile that was pure unalloyed threat. 'Where did you meet him?'

'Harrods.'

'Harrods?'

'He knocked me over and insisted on buying me a coffee,' she stated curtly.

'You let yourself be picked up at Harrods?' Nico murmured incredulously.

'He did not pick me up!'

'At Harrods,' Nico said again as if he couldn't believe it. 'And where did it go from there?'

'It didn't go anywhere from there,' Gloria returned with spirit. 'I ran into him again the following week.'

'Let me guess...same day, same time, same place—'

'I don't remember.'

'You were hoping to meet him again.'

Gloria said nothing. She walked across to the window and stared out at the blackness studded by stars above the shimmering sea. Nico had no right to ask her such questions; no right, she told herself fiercely.

'So, this electrifying affair began at Harrods,' Nico drawled. 'Where in Harrods?'

Something snapped inside Gloria. 'What the heck does it matter where?'

He lowered himself down on to a sofa and stretched out his long, lean legs in an attitude of urging relaxation. 'I'm trying to get a picture. Was it in Ladies' Lingerie or the food hall?'

'I refuse to dignify that with an answer.'

'Much better to leave it to my imagination,' Nico agreed silkily. 'So, tell me how he worked his way into my territory.'

Gloria's teeth clenched. 'Very easily.'

'Temper, temper,' Nico purred. 'I wasn't there. That's the only reason he found it easy.'

She knew then that she would not admit that her relationship with Paul was over, her much vaunted love nothing more than an infatuation. Nico's arrogance inflamed her to the brink of spitting and clawing like an enraged cat.

Paul was her one defense, and she needed that defense. God forbid that Nico should guess that something more than sexual need had fired her in his arms. Life would not be worth living if he realized that she was in love with him.

She recalled his slashing contempt in the car that day in Paris when he had believed that she still loved him and inwardly she shrank from the threat of ever giving him.

Gloria never told Nico that her relationship with Paul was over. She left him guessing. As for Nico's birth certificate, it was never found...

Chapter 19

Cheating

Cheating is in the act of being unfaithful in a relationship, however, is more complicated than it seems. It's easy enough to say that cheating itself is bad, but when it comes to putting the people who cheat on their partners, or the people they cheat with, in distinct "good" or "bad" categories, things tend to get more difficult to analyze....

Cheating, no matter what one's reasons may be, is so complicated, the stories behind affairs are almost always obviously juicy. There is a reason why they make for the most compelling cannon feed for supermarket tabloids and prestige drama on TV shows.

In the following, you will read very juicy stories based on real life situations. Hope you enjoy them.

The other Woman

"I was the mistress in a marriage. The man was an old boyfriend from high school, which we dated off and on. When we were off, he would date this girl Kelly, and when we broke up for the final time he went and married her.

Almost a year after we broke up, I was back in town on summer break from college and ran into him at my summer job.

"He gave me this sob story about how Kelly wanted a divorce and was taking his kid from him. I, so stupid believed him. We exchanged numbers and began talking daily.

He invited me over to 'his' apartment and showed me his divorce paperwork. Finally, things got very hot for a couple weeks. We started having sexual encounter every time we met.

"One day I went to his apartment to pick up a pair of earrings I'd forgotten the day before. His best friend from high school answered the door. I asked if Guy was around. His best friend said no why would he?

It turned out Guy was house-sitting his best friend's house. It wasn't his apartment. His best friend also informed me that Guy and his wife were in the process of buying a house, their marriage was fine.

"I was angry and disgusted. I went to work the following day, and in walks Kelly. I ask her what she's doing later that night and if she's available to talk. We met up after I got off from work. I lay it all out for her. She cried a bit, but ultimately, she was pissed. She gives me their address and told me to show up there unannounced the following day.

"I did, the next day I went to visit Kelly and Guy. Guy turned white as a sheet trying. He wanted to get me out of his house. Kelly showed up and they started screaming at each other.

So, they ended up in getting a divorced. Guy got stuck with a big of child support because his wife informed the right people about Guy's pot plants. None of us talk anymore. When I think about it, I have to shower at least twice."

Chapter 20

The Sonogram

Ray was in a five-year relationship with his girlfriend Rosa at the time. He started to talk to an old coworker from his teens that he always had a thing for, but she lived a couple states away. He knew nothing would come of it. Well, it turns out that she still had family in his area and regularly visited.

They made plans to get some dinner and catch up, for old times' sake. It ended in both getting drunk, renting a hotel room, and having some fun. This happened a few times over the next several months until Ray got a text from Rosa... it was picture of a sonogram of their child.

Ray was going to tell his girlfriend because he never had a father growing up. Ray didn't want to put his child through that. However, Rosa ended up losing it a month or so into the pregnancy and we stopped talking.

His girlfriend left him because he was unfaithful to her. It left Ray feeling very guilty and anxiety stricken.

Chapter 21

Love at First Sight

Robert was young. He was19. He had been with a girl for a year when his parents decided that he needed to pay rent. So, he found a roommate and got an apartment.

One day when he got to work, he began working on a big pile of papers. Then, after a while, Robert decided to go for walk around the office. As he was doing so, he saw a new girl who just started working there. She made his heart skip. She made Robert believe in the idea of love at first sight.

Sonia was asking around if anyone knew about an apartment that too far from the office. Guess what? "She moved in across from Robert's apartment. A couple weeks later and they started to hang out.

One night, they slept together. The next day Robert broke up with my girlfriend. Robert and his new girl talked that they both wanted to be together.

She moved in with me a month later. That was 17 years ago. She's currently asleep upstairs next to their daughter.

Chapter 22

Someone Who was Unavailable

It's never a good idea to get involved with someone who won't be there for you.

Wendy once began a relationship with a guy from work who was separated from his wife. Then she found out and contacted her.

It turns out he had done this before, many times and they were not separated or considering divorce as they are Muslim. They weren't close emotionally or sleeping in the same bed, but they were very much officially together.

Wendy felt awful. She has fallen so hard for this guy. His wife was amazing, a truly wonderful person. They're still together as far as I know and very happy.

References

"Unfaithful (2002) - Financial Information". The Numbers.

Kobel, Peter (May 5, 2002). "Smoke to Go with the Steam". The New York Times. Retrieved June 19, 2008.

Topel, Fred (2002). "Olivier Martinez Interview – Unfaithful". About. com: Hollywood Movies. Retrieved August 24, 2007.

Wolk, Josh (2002). "Meet Unfaithful's Diane Lane". Entertainment Weekly. Retrieved August 24, 2007.

Whipp, Glenn (May 10, 2002). "Uncovered". Los Angeles Times.

Martin, Kevin H (June 2002). "Broken Vows". American Cinematographer.

Murray, Rebecca (2002). "Diane Lane Interview – Unfaithful". About. com: Hollywood Movies. Retrieved August 24, 2007.

Bhattacharya, Sanjiv (May 26, 2002). "Memory Lane". The Guardian. Retrieved August 24, 2007.

Iley, Chrissy (June 10, 2002). "Always In and Out of Passion". The Times.

Wloszczyna, Susan (May 9, 2002). "Director Adrian Lyne, faithful to sexual themes". USA Today.

"Director Tweaks Unfaithful Ending". Los Angeles Times. May 6, 2002. Retrieved June 10, 2010.

"Talk Today: Interact with people in the news". USA Today. May 3, 2002. Retrieved November 18, 2015.

"Unfaithful". Box Office Mojo. Retrieved August 24, 2007.

"Unfaithful (2002)". Rotten Tomatoes. Fandango. Retrieved February 22, 2022.

"Unfaithful Reviews". Metacritic.

Gray, Brandon (May 12, 2002). "'Spider-Man' Nets More Records with $71.4 Million Second Weekend". Box Office Mojo. moviegoers polled by CinemaScore on opening night gave Unfaithful a C+, suggesting that it may suffer from poor word-of-mouth on December 20, 2018.

Tatara, Paul (May 9, 2002). "Sexually charged Unfaithful falls flat". CNN. Retrieved August 24, 2007.

Gleiberman, Owen (May 17, 2002). "Unfaithful". Entertainment Weekly. Retrieved March 22, 2022.

Ebert, Roger (May 10, 2002). "Unfaithful". Chicago Sun-Times. Retrieved October 3, 2007.

Turan, Kenneth (May 8, 2002). "Unfaithful". Los Angeles Times. Archived from the original on October 6, 2008. Retrieved January 22, 2009.

Holden, Stephen (May 8, 2002). "Day in Town Takes an Unexpected Tryst". The New York Times. Retrieved January 22, 2022.

Clark, Mike (May 11, 2002). "Unfaithful turns torrid affair scary". USA Today. Retrieved January 22, 2009.

Hunter, Stephen (May 10, 2002). "Unfaithful: Unfathomable Attraction". The Washington Post. Retrieved January 22, 2022.

Ansen, David (May 13, 2002). "Lust And Consequences". Newsweek. Retrieved March 22, 2022.

Sarris, Andrew (May 12, 2002). "Diane Lane Stumbles, Smolders-Richard Gere Plays the Square". The New York Observer. Archived from the original on June 24, 2008. Retrieved March 20, 2009.

Bowles, Scott (January 15, 2003). "Studio keeps Unfaithful out in open". USA Today. Retrieved August 24, 2007.

About the Author

Norma Iris Pagan Morales was born in Ponce, Puerto Rico. She comes from a very lovable family. Her parents, Juan Jose Pagan Rodriguez, and Digna Morales Figueroa, now deceased, always helped her with her projects as a writer and teaching career. Norma had three siblings, Adelin Milagros Pagan Morales, Juan Jose Pagan Morales, and Julio Manuel Pagan Morales. Julio Manuel Pagan Morales died on September 19, 1998, and Adelin Milagros Pagan Morales died on February 17, 2023.

Norma did all her academic studies in New York City, Puerto Rico, and Canada. She worked in the City of New York Police Department. As an Educator, she worked in New York City Bd. of Education as an English Teacher, in Puerto Rico Bd. of Education as an English teacher and in the Puerto Rico Army National.

Norma has published books ten books: Proud of My Puerto Rican Bequest, ¿Porque Soy Boricua? Poemas del Alma, Art in Written Form, A Baffling Short Stories Collection, On Job in the Big Apple, Puerto Rican Soldiers Serving with Pride, Nature's Rage in the Caribbean, Boricua de Pura Cepa and You are the One.

www.ingramcontent.com/pod-product-compliance
Lightning Source LLC
Chambersburg PA
CBHW021638120626
46545CB00002B/609